TRAPPED IN A
VIDEO GAME

BOOK FOUR

DUSTIN BRADY

CONTENTS

1. The Zipper — 1
2. Hide and Sneak — 7
3. Raul Ludbar — 13
4. Dead Drop — 19
5. Reactovision — 25
6. Blink and You'll Miss It — 33
7. Doom Island — 41
8. BUM-BUM — 47
9. They're Here — 53
10. Pee Butter Poopies — 61
11. Lions' Den — 69
12. Marshy Mallow's — 75
13. The Safe — 79
14. Spiky Dungeon — 85
15. Glitchquake — 89
16. Mr. Nice Guy — 95
17. No More Mr. Nice Guy — 103
18. Planet Bottomless Pit — 109
19. The White House — 115
20. Dodo Doody — 121
21. Sparky the Squirrel Saves the Day — 129
22. Escape — 135
23. Code Black — 141

OTHER BOOKS
BY DUSTIN BRADY

Trapped in a Video Game: Book One
Trapped in a Video Game: Book Two
Trapped in a Video Game: Book Three

Superhero for a Day: The Magic Magic Eight Ball

Who Stole Mr. T? Leila and Nugget Mystery #1
The Case with No Clues: Leila and Nugget Mystery #2

ACKNOWLEDGMENTS

Special thanks to Jesse Brady for the cover and interior illustrations. You can check out more of Jesse's sweet artwork on Instagram: @jessnetic.

PREFACE
In Case You Missed It

The only series anyone should ever start with the fourth entry is Star Wars. In fact, *Star Wars Episode IV* is so good that you don't even need to go back to Episodes I-III unless you really want to find out why everyone hates Jar Jar Binks so much. Trapped in a Video Game is not Star Wars. If you start Trapped in a Video Game with Book Four, you will be angry and confused and leave hurtful Amazon reviews. If it's been awhile since you've read the first three books, you can catch up by reading the following words scrolling through space:

A short time ago in this very galaxy, 12-year-old Jesse Rigsby got sucked into a video game. This was bad news for Jesse because he hated video games. Inside the video game, Jesse met up with his friend, Eric Conrad, and battled giant praying mantises, house-sized sand monsters and a super-powered alien known as the Hindenburg. Eric and Jesse finally escaped, but only because another kid from their class,

Mark Whitman, chose to take their place.

In *Trapped in a Video Game 2*, Jesse and Eric mounted a rescue mission by sneaking into the video game company Bionosoft through *Go Wild*, a mobile game kind of like *Pokemon Go*. After surviving attacks by a Bigfoot, a velociraptor and Bionosoft president Jevvry Delfino, Jesse, Eric and former Bionosoft employee Mr. Gregory pulled Mark out of his computer prison. Unfortunately, the rescue broke Bionosoft's system, which released everything else from their computers into the real world.

In *Trapped in a Video Game 3,* robots from one of Bionosoft's games started causing major damage in the real world after escaping their computers. In addition to transforming sewers, factories and amusement parks around town into deadly levels from their game, they also kidnapped Eric. Jesse teamed up with Mark, a friendly drone named Roger and an Australian girl named Sam to save Eric before the robots could blast him into outer space. After rescuing Eric, Mr. Gregory caught up to Jesse and asked if he'd said anything to anyone about men in suits working for "The Agency." That was strange, but not as strange as the information that Jesse got later from Mr. Gregory's son, Charlie. That wasn't Mr. Gregory, Charlie claimed. That was a robot lookalike. The real Mr. Gregory was missing.

CHAPTER ONE
The Zipper

"You want to see me throw up, don't you?"

"What? No! Come on, this is a fun ride!" I said as I pushed my friend, Eric, closer to the Zipper.

"It's definitely not fun, and it's barely a ride!" Eric said as he fought me. "It's a throw-up machine! A machine literally invented to make people throw up!"

Eric was right. The Zipper, if you're not familiar, is a carnival ride that tries to answer the question, "How many times will the human body handle being flipped upside-down in a single minute?" Its two-person spinning coffins are rickety and unpredictable and full of hard metal to slam your face into on your flipping journey. It is not a fun ride.

I smiled as I handed two tickets to the disinterested teenager in charge of the whirling death machine.

"Jesse! Are you listening to me?! Roger, talk some sense into him!"

beep beep bwyoooooop

Roger is a drone from the video game Super Bot World 3. After he got sucked into the real world through a computer glitch, he helped me rescue my friend Eric from the clutches of an enormous robot called Goliatron. If this is the first you're hearing of Roger, that sentence was probably the most confusing thing you've ever read, but I promise that it made sense at the time. Anyways, Roger got smashed to bits during the rescue, but our friend's dad, Mr. Gregory, rebuilt him from spare parts. Over the last few weeks, Roger has become our constant companion — always buzzing back and forth between my house and Eric's, never letting either of us out of his sight for long. We've become famous around the neighborhood for having a drone as a pet, and kids come from streets away now to watch us do tricks with him. Roger was doing one of those tricks now: wobbling back and forth while making a scary sound.

"See, Roger thinks it's a bad idea too," Eric said, trying to turn around.

"Roger, you hang out here. We'll be right back!" I grabbed the back of Eric's shirt and dragged him onto the Zipper. Eric tried to go limp, but it was too late. I'd wrangled him onto the ride.

"Good luck," the carnival worker said as he clicked our coffin door closed. Not "enjoy the ride," "have fun," or even "be safe." Good luck. I took a deep breath. We were going to need it.

The teenager returned to the control station and pushed the button to advance us upward and load the next coffin. Once we were in the air, I turned to Eric. "The reason I brought you on this ride is that I have something important to tell you, and I needed to do it in private."

"And you couldn't have done it in my room or your room or literally anywhere else besides the puke machine?"

"Listen, do you remember anything being off about Mr. Gregory after the whole robot thing?"

Eric wrinkled his nose. "I don't know, that was like two months ago. He's kind of a weird guy anyways, right? Isn't he always off?"

"Remember the first thing he asked us after we got rescued? He didn't ask if we were OK or what had happened or anything. He asked if we'd told anybody about 'The Agency.'"

"Yeah, so?"

"We didn't even know what The Agency was. Doesn't that seem weird when you think about it?"

"He was probably just trying to protect us from something."

"But what if he wasn't?"

Eric gave me a weird look. We creaked upward again as the teenager loaded another pod. I took a deep breath and told Eric about Charlie Gregory's theory that his dad wasn't really his dad, but instead, a robot made to look like his dad. I'd expected to spend most of the ride convincing Eric to believe this crazy idea, but he was on-board after just three sentences. Eric loves conspiracy theories.

"This is crazy!" Eric said. "Crazy!" His eyes widened while his mind worked overtime. The last pod finished loading, and the Zipper started spinning for real. "But, but why?"

"I'm guessing the suit people kidnapped the real Mr. Gregory and sent the robot lookalike to make sure we didn't say anything."

Eric tried to nod, but at this point, the Zipper had really kicked into gear, so his chin kind of just smooshed into his chest. Then he gasped. "Wait, so if Charlie's dad is actually a spybot..." Eric paused while we flipped four times in a row. "Then when he fixed Roger..." We flipped twice more. I waited for him to put it together. "Do you think he turned Roger into a spybot too?"

"That's what I think," I said.

Eric looked green. I couldn't tell if it was from the news or the flipping. "Why?" he croaked. "Why... did..."

Eric was really struggling, so I finished his sentence for him. "I don't know why they're spying on us. I think they just want to make sure we don't ruin whatever they have planned."

Eric grabbed my arm with one hand while clutching the bar with the other. "NO!" He looked at me with crazy eyes. "Why did you let me eat that elephant ear if you knew we were going on the Zipper?!"

"Oh. I didn't think about that. Sorry."

The Zipper finally, mercifully, slowed to a stop. "I assume you have some sort of a plan?" Eric mumbled with all the color drained from his face.

Oh yeah, I had a plan. I'd been working on it for weeks. I grinned. "I call it 'Operation: RMG' for Rescue Mr. Gregory. We're gonna get these guys. I'll tell you the whole plan, but..."

"BUT WHAT?!"

I looked out the door of our pod. Roger was staring back at us. He waved one of his little claws. "But we've gotta ride this again."

"I'm going to kill you."

CHAPTER TWO
Hide and Sneak

Two days later, Eric and I showed up at Charlie Gregory's house to start Operation: RMG with Phase One — Hide and Sneak. I'd barely slept all night and was already sweating. Eric, on the other hand, was grinning like he'd just won a trip to Disney World. I also noticed that he had on the dumb spy watch I'd told him not to bring.

When we got to the porch, Roger reached out his telescoping arm to ring the doorbell. A few seconds later, Mr. Gregory appeared. His face lit up when he saw us. "Jesse! Eric! It's good to see you again! And you too, Roger!" Roger beeped and did a little flip.

"Hey, Mr. Gregory!" Eric said. "Charlie invited us over to play hide-and-seek. Is he home?"

"He sure is! I'll grab him." Mr. Gregory took a few steps into the house, then turned around. "Can I get you two ice cream?"

"Yes! Please!" Eric said.

Mr. Gregory gave a thumbs up and a cheesy eyebrow wiggle, then disappeared into the house.

Eric glanced over with a "You sure this guy's a robot?" look. I stepped on his toe. Although this was Eric's first time at the Gregory house after learning the news, it was my fourth. The first time I came, I had the same reaction as Eric. After my chat with Charlie in the school bathroom, all I could picture were the Disney World Hall of Presidents animatronic robots with herky-jerky movements. But that's not what I got at all. On the surface, this new Mr. Gregory seemed just as normal as my own dad. He was warm and funny. He remembered things. One time, he even made a face like he got a brain freeze when he ate ice cream too fast.

But the more time I spent over Charlie's, the more weird things I noticed. For instance, Mr. Gregory seemed to be blinking harder than normal — as if he were trying to squeeze his eyes shut, if that makes sense. And then I noticed the timing of his blinks. When I started paying closer attention, I found that I could time each one to five seconds exactly. Five-four-three-two-one-BLINK,   five-four-three-two-one-BLINK. There were other things too. Like, he said "presumably" a lot. And he licked his finger before turning the page in whatever he was reading. And he always spent an extra-long time in the bathroom.

OK, OK, now that I write all those things down, they don't seem like the robot giveaways I thought they were at first. I guess they could all be weird adult things. But that's why we were here. Hide-and-seek is the best way to snoop through anyone's house. If Charlie's house held any evidence of robot activity, we'd find it and immediately bring it to the police.

To work together under the noses of Mr. Gregory and Roger, we established a few code words. "Pickles" was, "I'm fine." "Tuna" was, "I'm in trouble." And "mousetrap" was, "Get the robots out now because I found something big."

Charlie had a big, fake smile on his face when he came to the door. He seemed to be sweating just as hard as I was. "Hey, guys! Uh, pickles, huh?" (In retrospect, we probably should have come up with code words that'd be easier to use in normal conversation.) Charlie tried to do a complicated handshake with me, which failed miserably. I gave him the "play it cool" signal with my hands.

"Hey, do you want to play hide-and-seek?" I asked in a reading-from-the-cue-cards voice.

"Sure!" Charlie replied in an equally unnatural way.

"You guys had better watch out," Eric said. "I'm the hide-and-seek champion of the world."

Over the next half hour, Eric proved that statement to be maybe the least true thing he's ever said. Not only was he bad at snooping for robot stuff, he was bad at pretending to do anything but snoop for robot stuff. The first time I was it, I "found" Eric in the kitchen — not hiding in a cabinet or anything, but fumbling through the junk drawer. We eventually decided to make Eric the all-time seeker before he could blow it for the rest of us. Eric and Roger would look for Charlie and me, while the two of us would inspect every corner of the house.

Even with Eric out of the way, the investigation went poorly. It seemed like every time I got close to a possible clue, one of Charlie's little brothers or sisters would ruin it.

"HEY, WHATCHADOIN?!" little Cheyenne asked when she saw me picking through the wires behind the entertainment center.

"Shar warsh?" Christian asked, trying to hand me a lightsaber under the bed. "Shar warsh, shar warsh, shar warsh!"

"Ahhhhh ah ah ah AHHHHH!" the toddler screamed, blowing my cover inside the nursery.

So it came as no surprise when I found myself with a buddy in the bathroom. I was "hiding" in the tub, trying to peek down the drain (I was really running out of ideas) when the door shut. I rolled my eyes and sat still. As embarrassing as it'd be to reveal myself now, it'd be ten times worse if the other person in the bathroom happened to be a little kid who'd announce my presence to the whole house. I waited quietly for the sound of the toilet lid, but it never came. Instead, I heard someone picking through the medicine cabinet. That couldn't be a kid — the cabinet was too high. I silently peeked around the curtain.

It was Mr. Gregory. My heart raced as I slinked back until only the tiniest sliver of my face peeked out. He took something out of the cabinet. This could be it! I strained to get a better look. It was...

An electric shaver.

I rolled my eyes. Here I was, feeling like this important spy, and my big break was watching my friend's dad shave. I felt dumb.

Wait. What was he doing?

Mr. Gregory plugged in the razor, but instead of turning it on, he detached it from the power cord. Then he did something I'll never be able to erase from my mind.

He plugged the power cord into his skin.

CHAPTER THREE
Raul Ludbar

"TUNA!" the voice in my head screamed. "TUNA, TUNA, TUNA TIMES INFINITY!"

I wanted to run or throw up or both, but my body remained frozen as I watched Mr. Gregory pinch the skin of his left thumb and slowly pull it back from the nail to reveal a black socket underneath. Then he calmly plugged the cord into the socket. His mouth started moving. Slowly at first, then a million miles an hour. Right at the end, he did two things that I recognized — he jerked his hand into a thumbs up and wiggled his eyebrows. Wait, was he replaying the entire day? Maybe sending all his memories somewhere?

Immediately after the eyebrow wiggle, his eyes snapped super-duper wide open. I didn't mean to, but I let out a small gasp. Mr. Gregory stared into the mirror for a second, then slowly turned his head around. I quickly ducked behind the curtain. The curtain was just thin enough that I could see the outline of Mr. Gregory's head as he stared at the shower for a full ten seconds. I stopped breathing. If I could see him, did that mean he could see me? I prepared to scream "tuna" at the top of my lungs the second he opened the curtain. But he never did. Instead, he finally turned back around, put the cord back into the medicine cabinet and walked out of the bathroom.

As soon as he was gone, I gasped for air. We had what we needed. I waited a full minute, then snatched the cord from the medicine cabinet and sneaked out of the bathroom.

"SHAR WARSH?!"

I jumped a foot off the ground and spun around to see Christian standing there with his dumb lightsaber. "Not now!" I hissed. I ran down the stairs before any other little kids could blow this. When I got to the bottom of the stairs, I saw Eric in the kitchen eating ice cream, not even looking for us.

"Eric!" I gasped.

"Oh, sorry," he said. "Mrs. Gregory just came back from the store with ice cream. I probably should have told you, but it's Moose Tracks with fudge, and you know how I love to scrape the fudge off the top of that one."

"Where's Charlie?!"

"Like I said, I took a small break from looking to..."

Just then, Charlie walked into the kitchen. "What's going on?"

"Moose Tracks with fudge!" Eric said. "Your mom gets the good stuff!"

"It is good stuff, isn't it?" another voice said. Mr. Gregory rounded the corner.

I got goosebumps. "Guys, I really think..."

"Oh come on, Jesse, get over it. I'm sorry, OK?" Eric said. He turned to Charlie. "He's mad at me for eating ice cream instead of looking for you guys. But it's Moose Tracks with fudge, ya know? Jesse, I'll get it from the freezer for you guys. Just sit down and don't worry about a thing."

"OK, that's not it," I said.

"Then what is it?" Eric walked to the freezer. Before I could answer, Eric got distracted by something on the refrigerator door. "Hey, Charlie, who's Raul Ludbar?"

Charlie looked up with a start. "What?!"

Eric pointed to an invitation hanging on the fridge. "You got invited to a surprise party for someone named Raul Ludbar. That's not anyone in our class, right? I certainly didn't get invited to a party for Raul Ludbar. Did you get invited to a party for Raul Ludbar, Jesse?"

I couldn't take any more of Eric's babbling. I grabbed him by the shoulders and said, "Eric. Focus." When he shut up for two seconds, I stared him square in the eyes and asked, "Do you want to play Mousetrap?"

Eric looked confused. "Uh, the board game? No, not really."

I wanted to slap him so much. "MOUSETRAP."

Eric stared at me for a second before his expression changed. "Ohhhhh." Then he looked disappointed. "But... The ice cream."

"I'll put yours away in the freezer. OK?"

Eric sighed and turned around. "Mr. Gregory, Roger did this cool high dive loop thing before, and we were wondering how to make him do it again."

Mr. Gregory's face lit up. "Maneuver 459! That's a good one! I can show you in the backyard right now if you want!"

"That would be great," Eric said, even though his expression said otherwise.

Mr. Gregory and Eric walked outside with Roger zipping behind. When the door closed, I pulled the cord out of my pocket. "Charlie, look! This is what we need!"

"Great," Charlie said with a faraway look in his eyes.

"Your dad — or I guess not your dad, but that robot — pulled his own skin back and plugged this into his finger! It was the creepiest thing I've ever seen!"

"I'll bet," Charlie said, still staring through me at the refrigerator.

"Hey!" I tapped Charlie's head. "You OK? We

found what we need! Let's take this cord to the police and get your dad back!"

"We don't need to take that to the police."

I threw up my hands. "And why not?!"

Charlie didn't answer. I looked behind me to find out what had him so mesmerized. It was the invitation that Eric had mentioned earlier. I took a second look. The front of the invitation featured a cartoon robot holding balloons and a birthday cake. The robot had its finger in front of its mouth. "Shhh!" a speech bubble said. "It's a surprise!"

Charlie's hand trembled as he reached for the invitation. "I think my dad sent me a message."

CHAPTER FOUR
Dead Drop

Charlie wouldn't tell me anything else about the invitation that afternoon. All he'd say was that he needed to check something out, and he'd let me know more through a secret message the next day. So the following day, I brought Eric to the secret message spot — the wooden castle playground near our school.

On the way to the playground, Eric typed a message on his watch and showed me when Roger had his back turned. "This is why we all need spy watches."

I shook my head. Spy watches are great until a robot snatches one away and discovers the whole conversation. No, I wanted to do this right, and that meant dead drops. ("Dead drop" is an old-school spy term for leaving a secret message for another spy under the nose of the enemy. I probably could have just said that instead of using a phrase you didn't understand, but I wanted to show how much I know about spy stuff.)

To pull off this particular dead drop, Eric and I needed to play a game of tag. To review, hide-and-seek and playground tag were our two big spy moves. The CIA would have been proud. "You're it! Ready, set, go!" I yelled and raced to the playground.

Roger followed me until I got to the playground, then he raced back to Eric. He could fit inside the little crawling tubes, but he knew from experience that he was at risk of breaking one of his propellers if he got bumped in there. Once I reached the playground, I climbed up a ladder and dove inside the red crawling tube we'd agreed to use. Sure enough, an old piece of gum was stuck to the wall. I took three quick breaths to pump myself up and peeled the gross, chewed gum off the plastic. Behind the gum, Charlie had folded a small note with a five-word message.

"Come over. Now. NO ROGER."

My heart raced faster. I put the note back, crawled out of the tube and immediately let Eric catch me.

When he tagged me, I gave him a little nod to let him know he should check for a message. Then, I closed my eyes and started counting slowly. "One

Mississippi, two Mississippi…" While I counted, I started fiddling with a piece of candy in my pocket. I always have to fiddle with something while I'm thinking of a plan. No Roger. Just how were we supposed to do that? You can't run away from something that can fly, and Roger didn't have an "off" switch. When I finally got to ten, I started to turn around. "Ready or not, here I… AHHH!"

Eric was already standing face-to-face with me. "I got it," he said.

"You got what?!"

Eric winked, then announced loud enough for Roger to hear, "I'm bored with tag, wanna play with Roger for a bit?"

beeweepdiddywoop! Roger whistled and spinned.

"Come on," Eric said, "I'll show you the trick we learned yesterday!"

"What are you doing?" I whispered as we ran. "Did you see the note?" Eric winked again.

When we got to the edge of the park near the street, Eric turned to Roger and held out his palm. "Roger, come." Roger landed in Eric's palm. Eric then turned his back to the playground. "Watch this," he said with his eyes down the street.

I watched for a few seconds while Eric did

nothing. Finally, I gave up. "What are you waiting for?"

He licked his finger and held it up. "The winnnnnd," he said like he was Squanto or something. Finally, he was satisfied. "Ready, Roger?"

bloopity-bloopity.

"One... two... three!" Eric threw Roger at the sidewalk as hard as he could. Roger was up for the challenge — he put his little propellers into overdrive and pulled up an inch before he hit the concrete. Using the force from the throw as momentum, Roger zoomed as fast as I'd ever seen him go along the ground, into the street and up into a magnificent —

CRASH! CRUNCH! CRUNCH! CRUNCH!

Bus.

Roger was so focused on pulling into his loop that he didn't notice the quickly approaching bus. He splatted onto the windshield like a bug, then bounced a couple times onto the street.

"ERIC, WHAT DID YOU DO?!"

Eric looked quite pleased with himself. "Maneuver 459!"

"No, what you did was throw Roger into a bus! Which is something that's going to get us in big trouble with the suits!"

"Or it'll give us an excuse to go to Charlie's house so his fake dad can fix Roger. Which will give us plenty of time alone with Charlie."

That stopped my ranting right there. "Oh. That's actually a good idea."

Eric wiggled his eyebrows. "I know."

We picked as much of Roger's plastic and metal off the street as we could and dumped it into Eric's bookbag. Then we took off on our bikes. I turned around to make sure no suits had pulled into the parking lot or landed in a helicopter or something. We'd made it!

"Jesse, watch out!"

I turned back around and slammed on the brakes just in time to avoid a mom walking to the parking lot. She put her hand on my bike to keep me from running over her toes.

"I'm so sorry!" I said. "I should have been watching where I was going!"

The mom shook her head and continued walking to her minivan. I yelled another apology and caught up to Eric. If I'd been paying attention, I would have noticed something strange about the mom. She didn't have any kids with her.

CHAPTER FIVE
Reactovision

As we pedaled to Charlie's house, Eric reviewed the plan with me. "OK, so if the robot Mr. Gregory comes to the door…"

"Oh, we're calling him the RMG now," I interrupted.

Eric squinted at me. "I thought that was the name of the mission."

"It was, but I just changed it. Now it stands for 'Robot Mr. Gregory' because that takes too long to say."

"It doesn't take too long to say."

"It does! Also, the initials make him feel more like a robot. It seems icky to say 'Mr. Gregory' when we know that's not him. Just use the initials, OK?"

Eric rolled his eyes. "Fine, so if he comes to the door, we cry and cry about Roger being broken until Mr. Gregory…"

"The RMG!"

"Until the RMG volunteers to fix him."

"Yeah, except maybe we just ask nicely instead of crying. I think he can tell when we're faking."

"Don't worry. I can handle it," Eric assured me.

Five minutes later, Eric showed that we have very different definitions of "handling it."

"Mr. Gregory! Mr. Gregory!" he bawled before we even got to the door. I nudged him, but that only made him act harder. "Roger broke! OUR BEST FRIEND IS DEEEEEAAAAAAD!"

The RMG quickly opened the door. "Oh no! What part broke?"

Eric dumped his bookbag onto the porch. "All of them!"

The RMG's eyes got wide.

"He ran into a bus," Eric said, still trying to act sad, but clearly a little proud of himself.

"A bus?" The RMG stared at the parts in shock.

"Can you fix him?" I asked.

The RMG continued to stare. "I do have some spare parts in my workshop out back."

We picked up the pieces and followed the RMG

to a shed in the backyard. He turned on the lights to reveal shelves and workbenches lined with parts. He grabbed a flashlight and started picking through a bin. "PCFI capacitor, now where's the PCFI capacitor?" he muttered to himself.

"Uh, is this gonna be a while?" Eric asked.

"Presumably."

"Then we were gonna hang out with Charlie for a little bit if that's OK."

"Mm? Oh yes, of course," the RMG mumbled.

Charlie met us at the back door. His hair was all messed up, and he looked like he hadn't slept at all. "Did you get rid of him?"

Eric grinned. "Got rid of both of them!"

Charlie looked both ways. He was trembling. "Cool. Follow me."

We followed Charlie to the basement — a little kids' paradise packed with wall-to-wall toys. There was a stuffed animal classroom, a minefield of Legos and a sprawling Star Wars battlefield. I suddenly got nervous. "Wait, is your brother around?"

"He went with my mom and sisters to my grandparents' house," Charlie said as he picked his way across the room and opened a door. Once we all got inside, Charlie closed the door, locked it and clicked on a lamp.

"Whoa!" Eric and I said in unison. This smaller room was stuffed with a different type of toy — electronics. Mr. Gregory had guts of old computers strewn all over a table in the corner, tons of old video games lining shelves against the wall and a ratty couch facing a tube TV. Charlie turned on the TV and hit a switch on one of the video game systems.

The screen flickered a few times, and then video game music from the 80s greeted us as a title popped up — "DOOM ISLAND!" A blocky, little man swung back and forth on vines hanging off of the letters, while another character threw coconuts at a gorilla.

Eric's eyes lit up. "Is this what I think it is?!" Charlie didn't answer. Eric picked up one of the controllers almost reverently. "A Reactovision 9000. These are, like, super rare." Then his eyes got huge. "Can we play it? Can we play *Doom Island*?!"

I doubted Charlie had us go through all that trouble just to play an old video game. "What does this have to do with your dad, Charlie?"

Charlie took a few deep breaths to calm himself. "This is my dad's system from when he was a kid. He always said it's what made him want to start making video games. As soon as I got old enough to pick up a controller, we started playing *Doom Island* together. I still remember when we beat it for the first time. I actually hadn't thought about the game for years — that is until you guys pointed out the invitation on the fridge."

"The party for that kid we don't know?" Eric asked.

"Raul Ludbar," Charlie said. "That's the code my dad and I always used in *Doom Island* to get infinite lives."

"Ohhhhhhhh!" Eric said. Then he paused for a second. "Actually, I don't get it."

"You know how sometimes video games let you put in codes to get extra stuff?"

"Of course."

"Well, you put codes into Reactovision games through button combinations on the controller." Charlie grabbed the controller from Eric. "See, there's up, down, left, right, 'A' and 'B.' If you put in the right combo, you get cool stuff."

"Okayyyyy."

"The code for infinite lives in *Doom Island* is really complicated. Right-'A'-up-left-left, blah, blah, blah. It's really hard to remember unless you write it down, or…"

I was getting it now. "Or unless you come up with your own code!"

Charlie nodded. "Raul Ludbar isn't a name, it's a trick for remembering the *Doom Island* code. 'R' for right, 'A' for the 'A' button, 'U' for up."

Now I was getting excited. "So your dad was telling you to put that code into this game! And he wanted you to do it without telling anybody, which is why he sent the message through a surprise party invitation!"

Charlie nodded, then looked back at the door and slowly started punching buttons on the controller. Right, "A," up, left — Eric and I held our breaths until he hit the last button and a chime sounded. The screen turned black, and a message appeared on the screen one letter at a time.

ARE YOU ALONE?

- **YES**

- **NO**

Charlie selected "YES."

Another message typed onto the screen.

CHARLIE, YOU ARE BEING WATCHED. SOMETHING BAD IS ABOUT TO HAPPEN. GET THE FAMILY TO SAFETY BY BRINGING THEM INTO THIS ROOM AND TYPING THE CODE AGAIN.

LOVE,

DAD

We sat in silence for a moment. Charlie was still shaking. "Guys, what's going on?"

"Can I see the controller?" I asked. Charlie handed it to me, and I tried to scroll around the screen to look for any other clues. "Were there more instructions?"

Before Charlie could answer, the doorknob rattled. Charlie jumped to his feet. "Who is…"

The door swung open, and in stepped the RMG, holding a key.

CHAPTER SIX
Blink and You'll Miss It

"Hey guys, I fixed Roger!" the RMG said when he entered the room. Roger flew behind him and perched on his shoulder.

"That was — uh, fast," Eric said.

The RMG looked from me to Eric to Charlie to the TV. When he saw the TV, he stopped. His eyes didn't even move back and forth to read the text. He must have been able to read it all instantly, because the moment he saw it, his whole demeanor changed. His breathing slowed. He got cold. Robotic. He slowly swiveled his head to Charlie. "What's the code?" he asked in a flat voice.

Charlie looked like someone had kicked him in the stomach. "It's all part of the game."

"What's the code?" the RMG repeated in the same flat voice.

Charlie went silent. The only noise in the room

was the sound of heavy breathing.

The RMG blinked and tilted his head. "Charlie?" Then his eyes changed. They started getting brighter. Blink. Now they were turning red. Blink.

I looked around for an escape path. No windows, no other doors — the only way out was past the crazy-eyed death robot. Unless... I glanced at the controller in my hands.

"Roger," the RMG said without turning his head. "My son is having a hard time accessing his memories. Let's help him out."

Roger *bloop*ed and opened one of his belly compartments to reveal a spinning blade.

"Roger, no!" Eric yelled. He looked at me for help, but I couldn't take my focus off of the RMG's eyes. *Blink.* There it was. The instant he blinked, I pressed "right" on the control pad and started counting down.

5...4...3...2...1... *Blink.* I pressed "A" and started the countdown again.

Roger slowly buzzed toward Charlie, his blade whirring louder and louder. Charlie backed up until he hit the wall. It was horrific to watch, but I tried to stay calm and keep my eyes on the RMG. *Blink.* I pressed "up." I didn't know what the code did, but I knew it was our only chance. I also knew that if the RMG saw me type it in — even out of the corner of his eye — his robot brain could piece it together. So I stood there watching like a dummy while my friend stared down a head-sawing blade.

You know who didn't just stand there?

"Hey, ya dumb flying saucer! You want a piece of this?!"

Eric.

Roger ignored Eric, which turned out to be the wrong decision for the little drone. Just as Roger's spinning blade was about to reach Charlie's nose, a *CRACK* rang out, and Roger went flying. Eric had swung a Nintendo 64 controller with all his might and smacked the drone across the room. Roger spun into a lamp and sliced it in half with his still-spinning blade. Now, the only light in the room was coming from the TV. Roger righted himself and zoomed toward Eric, who was now holding an old computer tower like a shield.

"ERIC!" I screamed. Eric used the computer tower to smash Roger against the wall. That caused me to lose count. *Blink.* I missed my chance to hit the "down" button. I started counting again.

5...4...3...

Roger grabbed Eric's arm with his claw and brought it toward the saw.

...3...2...1... *Blink.* Down. I couldn't lose count again. This was Eric's only chance.

Shing!

Charlie threw an NES *Ninja Gaiden* game cartridge at Roger like a throwing star and hit one of his propellers. The impact threw Roger off balance, which gave Charlie an opportunity to pick up the next three games in the stack — *Tetris, Paper Boy* and *Bubble Bobble.*

Shing! Shing! Shing!

Each hit made Roger wobble and spin more. He even pulled in the blade so he could focus all his energy on righting himself. But Charlie didn't let up. He delivered the final blow with the *Super Mario Bros./Duck Hunt* combo cartridge, which caused Roger to tumble across the room and sputter in a heap at the RMG's feet.

The RMG looked down, unimpressed. Eric stepped forward. "That all you got?!"

The RMG smiled a creepy robot smile. Suddenly, his arm shot forward six feet and grabbed Eric by his shirt. I wanted to scream. I wanted to fight. I wanted to throw down the controller and punch the evil robot right in his face. But I couldn't. I was on the last blink.

...3...2...1... *Blink.*

I hit "right." The screen went black, and a new message appeared letter-by-letter.

EVERYONE HOLD THE CONTROLLER IN FIVE...

I glanced over. The RMG hadn't yet seen the message because he was staring at Eric with all the fury in the world. "You're not going to like what comes next," he said as he lifted Eric to the ceiling.

…FOUR…

A crash sounded upstairs by the front door. We heard people barrel into the house. "Down here!" the RMG yelled.

…THREE…

Still holding onto the controller, I grabbed Charlie's arm. "Charlie! Get Eric!"

…TWO…

Boots crashed down the stairs. Charlie lunged for Eric and yanked him out of the RMG's grasp.

…ONE…

Still holding onto the controller with my left hand, I pulled Charlie on top of me with my right. That pulled Eric on top of him, which flipped all three of us over the couch.

…GOODBYE.

Waswoooooosh!

Suddenly, my left hand felt like it was on fire. I tried to drop the controller, but I couldn't. My hand was frozen. Actually, my whole body was frozen. I struggled helplessly while the burning spread from my hand to my arm to my chest. The world began to fade as I started to fall.

There was noise. Lots of noise. I used all my

energy to focus on it. Near the door, a group of suits led by the "mom" I'd bumped into at the playground were all pointing at something. By now, my vision was almost completely black, but by squinting, I could start to see what they were pointing at. Another hand was feeling around near Eric's leg. A hand attached to a super-duper long arm.

"ERIIIII..." I never got to finish my warning. Because just then, everything disappeared.

CHAPTER SEVEN
Doom Island

Once I stopped falling, I paused for a moment to prepare myself. Then I opened my eyes, nodded and sighed. Just as I'd suspected. The world had turned blocky. It was like someone had built an entire jungle out of Legos — but not even normal Legos. It was like those big Legos they make for little kids. There were big, gray blocks that were supposed to be boulders, long, swinging blocks that were supposed to be vines, and little tan blocks at the end of my arms that were supposed to be...

"AHHHH!"

I screamed when I realized what those little tan blocks were. They were my hands. With no fingers. I tried to bring them to my face to get a better look, but I couldn't bend my elbows. I started to freak out. Not only was I apparently the only one who'd made the trip to Doom Island, but now I was going to be trapped here with no fingers, no elbows and no clue how to get out. Also, if that were true, it meant my friends were still stuck in the real world with the psycho robot. I stood up and ran back to look for a warp tunnel or something I could use to get back to them.

When I reached the boulder at the beginning of the level, I tried to climb over it. Turns out — and perhaps you've guessed this already — that climbing without fingers is basically impossible. I tried going around the rock. Nope. No matter how hard I tried, I could only walk forward and backward, not left or right. That's probably because *Doom Island* was a 2D side-scrolling game. I could walk anywhere I wanted in the other games because they were 3D like the real world. But in 2D, I could only walk back and forth, not side-to-side.

I finally tried jumping to see what was behind the boulder, and that's when I had my breakthrough. In this video game, I could jump a lot higher than I could in the real world. It felt like I was on the moon. I jumped all the way on top of the boulder only to find a black void behind it. No warp tunnel.

I tried putting my hand in my pocket to fiddle with something while I planned my next move, but of course, there was no pocket. All I could do was stare at the block jungle and think about how nice it'd be to not get sucked into a video game every other week. As I stared, I noticed something weird — a jumble of blocks started appearing below me. I crouched. Was this the first *Doom Island* enemy? More blocks joined the jumble. They got darker and began forming into a shape. Then I heard a chime, and suddenly the blocks joined together to make a person. I mean, not a normal person. Like, you know when your little brother draws a picture, and your mom goes, "Wow, what a great monkey, Joey!" and he says, "That's Batman." It looked kind of like that.

The Batman monkey stood up, stretched out his arms, looked down at his hands and screamed.

"Charlie!" I called out. "Is that you?"

Charlie looked up at the rock. "Jesse? What is this?!"

"*Doom Island.*"

"Obviously it's *Doom Island*! But, like, how?!"

I forgot this was Charlie's first time inside a video game. I hopped down from the rock. "It's that technology your dad invented that lets people go into video games. I think maybe he figured out a way to get your family into this game to keep you guys safe."

"WHY DOES YOUR MOUTH OPEN AND CLOSE LIKE PAC-MAN WHEN YOU TALK?!"

I don't think Charlie heard one word I said. I

grabbed him by the shoulder. Actually, I tried to grab him by the shoulder, but I really just set my big oven mitt hand on his shoulder, which I think freaked him out even more. "I don't know how it works. It just works, OK? Your dad knows what he's doing. Now, I need to know something — was Eric holding onto you when you got sucked in?"

"I-I don't... I don't..."

Charlie couldn't get the words out. I stared him in the eyes (actually, they were just two black dots so they could have been his nostrils) and took deep breaths with him to help him calm down. "Charlie, this is really important. If Eric wasn't holding onto you, then he's still in really big trouble."

"WHAT'S THAT?!" Charlie screamed, pointing over my shoulder.

I looked back to see a jumble of blocks and breathed a sigh of relief. I pushed Charlie back and said, "Watch." After a few seconds, the chime sounded, and those blocks pulled together into a third block person.

"YES!" Eric shouted with his Pac-Man mouth. He punched his fist in the air and jumped as high as he could. "I knew it, I knew it, I knew it!" He put his arms down and did a weird dance where the only things that moved were his hips going back and forth.

"Eric! I didn't know if you'd made it! I saw the RMG reaching for you." I tried to walk around Charlie to hug Eric, but I couldn't, so I settled for jumping and high fiving him over Charlie's head.

"Pshhh, that guy?" Eric said. "He was nothing. He yanked at me the whole time, but he was no match for these." He tried to make a muscle, but of course, his elbow wouldn't move.

"The whole time?" I asked.

"Right up until the end."

"You shook him off though, right?"

"I kicked him a whole bunch."

"That's not what I asked," I said as my heart started racing again. "Did. You. Shake. Him. Off?"

"Uhhhh…"

Eric didn't need to answer. Because the two eye dots on Charlie's face got really wide at that moment. He pointed over my shoulder. I turned around to see a massive jumble of blocks form right behind me.

CHAPTER EIGHT
BUM-BUM

"RUN, RUN, RUN!"

I ran into Charlie who ran into Eric who just stood there staring at the block blob. "What's that?"

Charlie pushed Eric. "IT'S GONNA KILL US!"

"It's the RMG!" I yelled. "He got in because he was holding your foot when the controller zapped us. Now move!"

Eric finally understood and sprinted into the jungle. Charlie followed close behind, and I suddenly realized that being the last in line would make me first to get snatched by the RMG. "Can we pick up the pace?" I yelled ahead to Eric.

Charlie also had some advice for Eric. "OK, if I remember right, the first enemy will look scary, but it's not that bad. All you have to do is jump, and..."

DING!

Oh no. I put my hand on Charlie's shoulder. "He's here," I whispered. "Let's keep it down."

"AHH!" Eric screamed, doing the exact opposite of keeping it down.

"Eric, shut... AHH!" Even though I knew the danger of alerting the RMG by screaming, I couldn't help myself. A four-foot-tall snake standing in a striking cobra pose was barreling toward us. Now, I know snakes usually slither or squirm, not barrel, but this one was definitely barreling, almost like it was on wheels.

"JUMP!" Charlie yelled, just before the snake reached us. All three of us cleared the snake easily. I turned around to get another look at the snake, and that's when I caught my first glimpse of the RMG. The transfer to digital did not treat him kindly. The video game version of the RMG had no human skin. All that remained was a gray robot skeleton and a pair of red, glowing eyes. Even though the eyes were little more than two red dots, they were somehow still filled with hate. When his two red dots made eye contact with my two black dots, he started running faster.

"Guys, he's..."

BUM-BUM

The RMG didn't even try to avoid the snake. He ran right into it, causing him to turn red then disappear, making the *BUM-BUM* sound.

"Did he just die?" I asked.

"Yeah, but he's not gone for good," Charlie said. "He just went back to the beginning of the level."

"We know the drill," Eric said. "This isn't our first time inside a video game, ya know." Then Eric motioned for Charlie to jump ahead of him.

Over the next few minutes, Charlie led us over a bunch more snakes, showed us how to cross a river by using snapping crocodile heads as springboards and helped us dodge divebombing toucans. I kept looking over my shoulder for the RMG, but he hadn't caught up yet. Eventually, we reached a pit with a vine swinging over it. Charlie ran to the edge, looked down, nodded, then backed up. He took a running start and leaped for the vine just as it reached our ledge. He held onto it for a few swings, then jumped ahead when the vine reached a moving platform. He turned around. "Go ahead, grab on!"

Eric held out his hands. "With what?! We don't have fingers!"

"Your hands are like magnets," Charlie said. "It just works!"

Eric nodded and backed up like Charlie had done. When the vine got close, he started running, but slammed on the brakes before he got to the edge. "Sorry." He backed up to try again.

I glanced nervously over my shoulder.

Eric made the jump on his second try, but he held onto the vine too long to get to the moving platform right away. He climbed to the top of the vine to get a better angle.

"You need to go back down," Charlie said.

"It's an easier jump from the top," Eric replied. "This is how I always do it in video games."

"No, you need the momentum from the bottom!"

"I'll bet you a hundred bucks..."

"SHUT UP AND JUMP!" I yelled. I'm not normally one to yell "shut up" at people, but I'd just spotted a crocodile flinging a death robot into the air behind us.

"You know what, Charlie, you might be right this time," Eric said, still oblivious. "It does seem like you need to be at the bottom of the vine in this game."

"HE'S RIGHT HERE!"

Eric looked over his shoulder to finally see the RMG closing in on us. "Oh!" He held onto the vine one-two-three more swings and jumped as soon as the moving platform was in reach.

I sneaked a peek behind my shoulder. The RMG was right there. Just before he could grab me, I jumped. The vine was still far away, but I flew faster and farther than I'd expected. Maybe I could make it! I reached as far as I could and got super-duper close to touching the vine. Unfortunately, "close" is not good enough on Doom Island. The vine passed just overhead, and I tumbled into the pit.

BUM-BUM

CHAPTER NINE
They're Here

I opened my eyes in a panic at the beginning of the level. My only hope of safety was sticking with Eric and Charlie, and now an angry, red-eyed robot stood between us. Before I could start to figure out my next move, I heard another *BUM-BUM*.

This was it. The RMG had followed me down the pit. I started to run, but the thing grabbed my shoulder.

"Hey, over here."

I turned around. It was Charlie.

BUM-BUM

And Eric.

"Quick, follow me," Charlie said as he jumped onto the boulder at the beginning of the level. Eric and I scrambled after him. Since the boulder only had enough room for one person, we ended up standing on top of each other's heads to make a human totem pole. Then, the bottom of the totem pole started doing a weird dance.

"Cool it!" Eric said. "You're gonna make us fall off!"

But that's not what happened. Instead, Charlie completed his dance and disappeared behind the rock.

"How did you do that?!" Eric asked.

"Duck three times and look up once!" Charlie answered. "It's a secret in the game to get a prize."

Eric tried the move, and sure enough, he fell behind the rock too.

"This is so cool!" I heard Eric say. Then I heard another sound.

BUM-BUM

The RMG had finally taken the plunge down the pit.

I managed to duck twice before the RMG showed up looking angry and confused. I quickly ducked again, looked up and fell behind the rock.

From behind the rock, I peeked at the RMG. We could see him, but he couldn't see us. Right now, he was looking the rock up and down. "Do you think he saw me?" I whispered to Eric.

Eric responded by holding up a glowing orb in glee. He'd found the prize behind the rock, and he couldn't be happier. I reached out to touch the orb, and like a little kid, Eric yanked it away and held it tight to his chest. As soon as the orb touched his chest, it absorbed into Eric's body, turning him bright white. He started flashing, and loud, happy music began playing.

Dodo doody doodoo doody-doody

"STOP IT!" I mouthed.

Eric threw up his hands. There wasn't anything he could do. His body continued producing obnoxiously loud music all by itself.

Dodo doody doodoo doody-doody

Our rock now had the RMG's full attention. He turned, stared at it, then jumped on top and tried looking down. We all crouched lower. He examined the rock from all angles, then tried tapping it with his robot claw. Finally, his eyes got super bright and shot lasers at the rock, which was a terrifying thing that I didn't even know was a possibility.

Finally, Eric's body stopped flashing and singing. We all remained still. The RMG did a few more rounds before disappearing into the jungle. After a full minute, we let ourselves breathe again. "What just happened?!" Eric asked.

"That was an invincibility orb," Charlie said. "It's a pretty good prize as long as you're not trying to hide from a murder robot."

I looked out at the jungle. "Unfortunately, the murder robot is still out there."

"Pssssssssssst."

"What do you want, Eric?" I asked while still keeping an eye on the jungle.

"Psssssssssssst."

"Come on, spit it out. I'm in no mood."

"PSSSSSSSSSSSSST."

"WHAT?!" I turned around to see that Eric could not have made the "psst" sound because Charlie had his hand over his mouth. Charlie may have made the sound, but I would bet a lot of money that it was the giant snake hovering over Charlie's shoulder. I started to scream, and Eric put his hand over my mouth.

The snake looked like one of the cobras-on-wheels that had been chasing us earlier, but this one was bigger. Much bigger. It looked like one of those blow-up animals they put on top of car dealerships to announce sales, except if the dealership were super weird and decided that an evil, black snake would help them sell more cars. This snake floated in the darkness behind the level and stared at us. I waited for it to eat us all with one bite. Finally, it opened its mouth. I cringed. But instead of lunging, it spoke.

"Hi."

The voice was really strange. I know I should have been more freaked out by a giant video game snake talking to me in the first place, but I just couldn't get over the voice. It was like Elmer Fudd crossed with Winnie the Pooh. We all looked at each other. Finally, Eric responded. "Hi, Talking Snake."

"Charlie," the snake said. "This is your dad."

Should it have surprised me that a digital talking snake was claiming to be Charlie's dad? Of course. It is impossible for a video game snake to be anyone's dad, except maybe a baby video game snake. However, after all the things I'd already seen, I was not surprised even a little bit. Charlie, on the other hand, looked like his mind had exploded.

"Uh, hi," Charlie said.

"Charlie, I'm so glad you're safe," the snake continued. "I can't see you — I'm typing all this on a computer. Is the family with you?"

"Dad, where are you?"

"I'm fine," the snake said. "Just, please tell me the

family is all there safe with you."

"Dad, I'm so sorry. The robot was coming, and…"

Charlie couldn't bring himself to finish the sentence, so I did. "I put in the code early," I said.

"Who's that?" the snake asked.

"It's Jesse Rigsby. I pulled Charlie and Eric into the game because the robot was about to kill us."

The snake went silent. I imagined Mr. Gregory trying to process everything I'd just told him.

"I'm really sorry," I said. "It was the only thing I could think of in the moment. Roger was about to chop off Charlie's nose, and then the robot version of you was looking at Eric with these scary, red eyes, and…"

"Does he know you're here," the snake interrupted.

"Who? The robot?"

"He's in here with us," Eric said.

"Now?" the snake asked. "Right now?!"

Even though the snake couldn't change its expression, I felt the panic coming from Mr. Gregory.

"Yeah," I whispered.

"Then they know," the snake said to itself. "They'll be here any second."

"Who will be where? How do we get back out?"

"You get out by beating the game, but that's not safe," the snake said. "You have to..." The snake froze.

"We have to what?!"

Suddenly, the snake *bloop*ed and started disappearing and reappearing. It tried to say something every time it reappeared. "TH-TH-TH-TH-TH..."

We all leaned in closer. "What is it?!"

Suddenly, the blinking stopped. The snake was gone. We all stared into the blackness for a while wondering what to do. Then, the snake reappeared for just a moment to whisper a two-word message.

"They're here."

CHAPTER TEN
Pee Butter Poopies

"Who's here?!" I whipped my head back to the jungle. I didn't see anyone.

"Hey guys," Charlie said. "Do you think we shooooooo…"

"Charlie, are you OK?" I spun around to see that Charlie had frozen in place. His eyes looked panicked, but his mouth wouldn't move. He continued to "oooooo." Then I noticed that the black edge of the level had begun to creep forward and was currently covering part of Charlie's left hand. "Help him!" I yelled, pointing at the hand. Eric quickly yanked Charlie away.

As soon as Charlie broke free from the blackness, he gulped for breath. "I couldn't move a muscle!" Then he looked down at his video game hand — or rather, half a video game hand. The part that had been covered in blackness was now gone. "WHAT HAPPENED TO MY HAND?!"

"Does it hurt?" Eric asked.

Charlie took a second to breathe. "No." He examined his half-hand. "No, it doesn't. It just looks like a spatula. Is it gonna grow back?"

I was too busy staring at the blackness to answer. Eric had pulled Charlie a good five feet away from the edge, but now the edge seemed to be creeping toward us. "I don't think we can stay here," I said. Eric and Charlie both looked up, noticed the same thing I did and took off into the jungle.

"Is the RMG doing this?" Eric asked as we hurdled the first two snakes.

"That's my guess," I answered, ducking underneath a toucan. As we ran through the level, I worked on a new plan. Inside the video game or out in the real world, our goal remained the same — rescue Mr. Gregory. But we couldn't do much to help him if we were constantly running from the RMG. My mind raced to figure out a way to take him out. Charlie interrupted my thoughts by screeching to a halt right in front of me.

"We've got a problem," he said.

I looked ahead to see that we'd made it back to the swinging vine. Charlie held up his spatula hand. "I don't think I can grab anything with this," he said.

"You don't know unless you try," Eric suggested.

"Yeah, but if it doesn't work, then I go back to the beginning of the level, right? Well, that's gone. If I die now, I'll probably be gone for good."

We stood in silence for a few moments. Finally, Eric picked up Charlie.

"What are you doing?" Charlie asked.

"Remember the guy throwing coconuts on the title screen when you turned on the game in your basement? I'll bet I can throw you across the pit!"

"I'm not a coconut!"

"Eric, I don't..."

Before I could finish my objection, Eric hurled Charlie across the pit like King Kong. "Did you see that?! THAT WAS AWESOME!"

"Eric, you can't do stuff like that on your own," I lectured.

"It worked, didn't it? I just... Hey. Where's Charlie?"

I looked across the pit. Charlie was gone.

"CHARLIE!" I screamed in panic.

Charlie poked his head out from behind a rock. "Over here! Sorry, I was just getting the extra life behind this rock."

Eric and I swung over the pit to catch up with Charlie. Once we did, Eric pointed to a cave opening up ahead. "What's that?"

"The entrance to the second level!" Charlie said.

"Sweet!" Eric started walking toward the cave.

"Wait," I warned. "We haven't seen the RMG yet."

"Right."

"What if he's pushing us toward the cave? What if he's waiting for us in there so he can pick us off one-by-one?"

That stopped Charlie. He thought for a second. "Then what are we supposed to do?"

"What if we get him to come to us instead?" I explained my plan. Eric and I could hide behind the rock while Charlie poked his head into the cave to lure out the RMG. Charlie would then lead the RMG to the edge of the pit, and at the last second, I'd throw Eric into the RMG, knocking him into the pit.

"I have another idea," a voice said behind us.

We all spun around. The snake had returned. "Snake Mr. Gregory!" Eric yelled.

"We don't have much time," the snake said. He motioned with his head, and a door appeared. "You need to get in here."

Eric started to walk to the door. I grabbed him before he could open it. "The RMG is gone, and now you show up," I said to the snake. "How do we know you're really Mr. Gregory?"

"Please go through the door," the snake said. "They could find this any second."

That was not the reassuring answer we were looking for. "I think you need to tell us more than that," Charlie said.

"Charlie, listen," the snake replied. "I'm helping the bad guys for now, which means..."

"You're doing what?!" Charlie yelped.

"For now!" the snake repeated. "They've locked me in this office building, and they keep threatening to hurt you and the family. To protect you, I built *Doom Island* level-by-level on different computers around here behind their backs. I thought that hiding you inside the game would finally give me the chance to destroy the thing they're making me build, but all it did was trap you in a world that they can erase with one keystroke. They're working on doing that right now."

"Is that why everything is disappearing behind us?" I asked.

"Yes, but only the first level. They found that one because I kept it on a computer I work on all the time, but there's another level farther in the game that they don't know about yet. This door is a shortcut to that level. Please. Walk inside. You can get to a safe…" The snake stopped talking.

"A safe what?" Eric asked.

I shook my head. I had no idea if we could trust the snake, but we had to make a decision fast. The darkness had already caught up to the pit. "Can you prove to us that you're really Mr. Gregory?" I asked.

The snake nodded. "Pee butter poopies."

"Uh okayyyyy," Eric finally said. "Thank you, Mr. Snake. That was very helpful, but…"

"Pee butter poopies," the snake repeated. "Charlie, you remember."

Charlie nodded. "The first time my dad and I beat *Doom Island* together, we went out for ice cream. I wanted the peanut butter chocolate chunk ice cream, but I couldn't really say 'peanut butter,' and I thought that the chocolate chunks looked like little poops. So I stood at the counter repeating 'pee butter poopies' a bunch of times until my dad figured it out. We still laugh about it now." A small block tear appeared on Charlie's face.

I put my hand on Charlie's shoulder. "Charlie, maybe that is your dad. But even if it is, going through that door just keeps us safe — it doesn't help him or your family. If we follow my plan, we can take out the RMG and still have time to rescue your dad."

"I trust my dad," Charlie said.

"I didn't say I don't trust him. I just think we need to stick to the plan."

Charlie turned to the snake. "Love you, Dad."

"Love you lots, kiddo," the snake replied.

With that, Charlie opened the door and walked inside.

"Charlie, wait!" I tried to reach through the door to grab him, but it was too late. I looked back to see that the darkness had finished crossing the pit.

"What are we going to do?" Eric asked.

What else could we do? Charlie had left us no choice. I followed Charlie through the door.

CHAPTER ELEVEN
Lions' Den

As soon as I stepped through the door, I started floating. Whoa. I grabbed for the handle to force my feet back to the ground, but the handle had disappeared. In fact, everything was gone except for blue stuff and colorful trees. Blue stuff and colorful trees? Suddenly, everything made sense. Water and coral! We were underwater!

I panicked and swam upward as fast as I could, only to discover a ceiling. An underwater cave?! My lungs began to burn as I clawed along the ceiling, desperately searching for air pockets.

"Jesse!" Eric yelled behind me. I stopped struggling for a second. During the summer, Eric and I play a game at the pool where one person sings something underwater, and the other guesses the song. Eric does the same thing every time, "Blub blub blubbity-blub," and then tries to claim that it's everything from Jingle Bells to the National Anthem.

But this time, his underwater voice sounded crystal clear. Almost normal. I spun around. Eric and Charlie were calmly floating behind me wearing snorkels and flippers.

"You can breathe down here," Charlie said, tapping his snorkel.

I reached up and felt a snorkel in my own mouth. I shook my head. Nope, nope, nope. Snorkels have to be sticking out of the water to work. I wasn't stupid.

"It's an old video game," Charlie assured me. "It's not realistic."

I finally took a breath — not so much because I trusted Charlie, but because I was about to pass out.

"See?" Charlie said. "Pretty cool."

Now that I could finally breathe, I took the opportunity to yell at Charlie. "What would be pretty cool is if you'd include us in your decisions instead of going off on your own!"

"I wasn't going off on my own," Charlie shot back. "I was leading the group!"

"Well, you just led us away from our only chance to save your dad!"

"Hey, Jesse," Eric said. "Chill. We'll figure out a way to help Mr. Gregory from here, OK?" He turned to Charlie. "As long as we're down here, mind showing us around?"

Charlie took a second to settle down and nodded. "This is actually a pretty cool level. Follow me."

I stopped for a few deep breaths, then fell in line for the tour. As long as we were here, might as well make the most of it. After all, how many times do you get to breathe underwater?

Charlie turned around. "Watch out for..."

Just then, a blocky, gray shark-shaped blob shot out of a hole below us. Without missing a beat, Charlie aimed his snorkel at it and blew a bubble. When the bubble hit the creature, it blinked red and disappeared.

"Wait, did you just kill a shark by blowing a bubble at it?!" Eric asked.

"It was 1986. I don't think they tried too hard to make any of this make sense," Charlie said.

Eric shook his head. "Even so..."

We bubble-blasted two more sharks and a swordfish before Charlie pointed out a treasure chest. "Check it out," he said. "Jesse, do you want the invincibility orb this time?"

I understood that Charlie was trying to be nice to

me to smooth things over from earlier, and I appreciated the gesture. I swam down and opened the chest. But instead of a finding a glowing circle inside, I found a piece of paper. I picked it up.

"Charlie," I read aloud. "I need to tell you what's going on in case I don't make it." I looked around.

"What does the rest of the note say?" Eric asked.

"That's it."

"Maybe the rest of the message is in the other treasure chests!" Charlie suggested.

We swam as fast as we could to the next treasure chest. Charlie opened this one. "Max Reuben is the man who kidnapped me." Charlie looked up, confused. "Is that the guy from *Lions' Den*?"

I was just as confused as Charlie. "Yeah, I think so." I shook my head. "This is so weird. I know he's really mean on the show, but it's just a show, right?"

"What show?" Eric asked. "What's *Lions' Den*?"

"It's a *Shark Tank* ripoff where billionaires give money to inventors," I answered. As we swam to the next treasure chest, Charlie and I explained that Max Reuben was a billionaire on the show who'd nicknamed himself "Mr. Nice Guy" as a joke because he was always the meanest. He'd offer deals then take them back just to be cruel. He'd make fun of people.

One time, he even broke a guy's invention on purpose. It always seemed like he was auditioning for the role of a supervillain in a comic book movie or at least a spot on *Shark Tank*.

Charlie cleared out a few squids with his snorkel before opening the next treasure chest. "Max has an evil plan for my technology."

"What's the plan?!" Eric complained. "Come on, are we going to have to open 200 more treasure chests to get this whole message?"

"Be patient," Charlie said before squeezing through a small opening in the wall. Eric and I followed. The opening sucked us through a series of tubes before dumping us into a small, dark room with a treasure chest at the bottom. "Here we go," I said as I swam down and opened it.

It was empty.

"Maybe the paper fell out somewhere," Charlie suggested. He looked next to the treasure chest, while I felt around inside.

When I reached into the chest, I looked down and noticed my hand. It had fingers. I held it up to my face. That's when I noticed something even weirder. I could bend my elbow now. "Guys, what's going on?"

Charlie turned and gasped. That made Eric turn. He screamed. "You're turning back to normal!" Charlie said.

I noticed that skin was spreading from the hand that had been inside the treasure chest to the rest of my body. My chest got heavy as it turned from blocks to normal clothes. The water suddenly felt cold against my skin. I took a couple big breaths, then sucked a few drops of water into my nose. I opened my mouth to take another big gulp, and water rushed in.

I couldn't breathe underwater anymore.

CHAPTER TWELVE
Marshy Mallow's

As soon as Charlie figured out what was going on, he hooked his block arm around my real one and pulled me into another tube. We quickly popped out the other side and started swimming like crazy. Eric sped ahead and began clearing out enemies with his snorkel. Swordfish. Gone. Octopus. Gone. Shark...

Uh oh.

This shark wasn't a block blob anymore. It had real skin, real eyes and super-real teeth. It also didn't look like the type of creature that could get killed by a few bubbles in the face.

"Swim faster!" Charlie screamed.

Eric did an underwater flip over the shark. But the shark wasn't worried about Eric. It had its eyes on Charlie and me.

"Stick together," Charlie whispered as we swam closer. "Stick together, stick together, stick together…" He held me underneath his body until we were just a foot from the shark. The shark lunged. "SPLIT!" Charlie pushed me underneath the shark, while he swam over it.

"GO, GO, GO!"

We caught up to Eric, and Charlie led us to another crack in the rock wall. Eric squeezed in, then Charlie followed. By now, my lungs were burning. This was the longest I'd ever held my breath. I swam for the crack and sneaked a peek behind me just in time to see the shark lunge. I used the last of my energy (and the last of my oxygen) to make a final kick for the crack. The shark took one of my flippers, but I slipped through before he could get me.

As the current sucked me through the tubes, I tried to think of anything besides the fire in my lungs. Fire… Fire… Fire… Marshmallows! I could think about marshmallows! You make marshmallows over a fire. I'm a really good marshmallow chef. Eric always turns his into a flaming torch, but mine come out golden brown every time. I should charge money for my marshmallows. Maybe open a grilled marshmallow restaurant. Call it Marshy Mallow's. There could be a big marshmallow mascot named Marshy walking around performing magic and giving marshmallow-shaped balloons to kids. That would be nice.

The more I thought about my award-winning restaurant, the groggier and loopier I got. The world started turning black. Suddenly, everything snapped into focus again when I saw a fork in the tunnel coming up. I could choose to go up or down. Up or down, up or down? I decided on up. Up is where dry land is.

But just as I started angling my body upward to take the top tube, I noticed something coming toward me from the bottom tube. Marshmallows. Hm. Weird that I'd just been thinking about marshmallows, and here they were. Maybe I could eat one.

Wait! Those weren't marshmallows at all! They were air bubbles. Probably air bubbles from my two friends with unlimited oxygen. I needed to change course. Fast. With half my body already in the top tube, I swung my legs into the bottom tube. For a second, I stayed like that — the current pinning me against the divide. Then, after the longest second of my life, I slipped down into the bottom tube.

I relaxed again. As I slid along the tube, the burning in my lungs went away. My chest just felt heavy. Everything faded again. I was vaguely aware of my body shooting out of the tube into another underwater chamber. I think something grabbed my ankle. Finally, everything went black for good.

CHAPTER THIRTEEN
The Safe

When I finally re-opened my eyes, I saw that I was now lying on the ground. The world had gone from blue to orange. I tried breathing. Success! Wait, had I actually made it back to the real world? I quickly raised my hands to my face, then sighed. Oven mitts.

"He's not dead! He's not dead!" Eric and Charlie high-fived oven mitts over my body.

"What happened?" I asked as I sat up.

"It was all Charlie!" Eric exclaimed. "You were pretty much toast, but he put his snorkel into your mouth and gave you air until we finished the level!"

"But how did you..." I looked back down at my oven mitts. "Why am I a video game character again?"

Eric shrugged. "As soon as we got to this level, you changed back."

Charlie explained further. "I think the bad guys probably found the water level computer and started messing with the code."

I looked around to see that we were inside another cave, but this one had fire everywhere. "So are we just going to keep running from level to level until they kill us for good?"

"No," Charlie said. "For one thing, there aren't many levels left. This is the second-to-last one. But more importantly, I just realized my dad told us where we can finally be safe."

"Yeah, it was that level where Jesse almost drowned," Eric asked.

"No. The safe."

"He never said anything about a safe," Eric said.

"He did. Remember when he told us to walk through the door? He said we could get to 'a safe'? The way he said it made it sound like he'd gotten interrupted, but I just realized that he was telling us to go inside the safe at the end of this level."

"Can you tell us a little more about this safe?" I asked.

"The first time we played this level, my dad showed me a secret passage he'd found. It's so secret that he'd never seen another person talk about it. He didn't even think the game developers knew about it. Anyways, if you jump at just the right spot and then quickly crouch-walk, you can pass through a spot in the wall and then fall into a huge pit of prizes. The only problem is you can't get back out. That's why we called it, 'the safe.'"

"That sounds bad," Eric said.

"It is if you're trying to beat the game. But not if you're trying to stay safe."

"We're not doing that," I said.

"What?" Charlie spun around.

I stood up. "Our goal is to get out of the game. We're not getting trapped in some room when the end of the game is right there."

"We're not trapped if my dad has a plan. If he thinks that's the best place for us, then that's where we need to be."

"Charlie, listen. Your dad is a super nice guy. But so far, everything he's done to keep us safe has backfired big time. Maybe he just keeps putting us in video games because it's all he knows. Maybe there's a better way."

Charlie got in my face. His voice was a little shaky. "My dad knows more than all three of us combined will ever know. Don't talk, about him like that. Ever. You don't understand what he's going through right now."

I tried to use my calming voice. "And you don't understand what we've been through. This is my fourth video game. I've nearly been drowned, crushed and sliced to death, all thanks to your dad. I'm just tired of it. Maybe it's time…"

BUM-BUM

Charlie interrupted my speech by pushing me. The shove caught me by surprise, and I stumbled backward onto a red square. As soon as I touched the square, a fireball shot from the ground and killed me.

When I reappeared, I started marching toward Charlie with my finger pointed at him. "You want to play like that?!" Charlie looked scared. Good.

"Hey, hey. Calm down." Eric started jogging toward me.

"ERIC, STOP!" Charlie yelled.

BUM-BUM

Too late. Eric got vaporized by a dive-bombing, fire-breathing bat. He reappeared next to me.

"STOP!" Charlie shouted in panic. "DON'T MOVE!" He looked distraught. "You only get three lives in this game. You both have used two now."

"Uh, what happens when you use all three lives?" Eric asked.

"You — you go back to the beginning of the game."

"Which doesn't exist anymore," I finished.

All three of us stood in silence for a few seconds. Charlie looked like he was going to cry. "I'm so sorry for doing that," he finally said. "It's just — I know my dad is doing everything he can to help us right now, ya know?"

"I know."

"He trusted me, and then I let him down by not rescuing my family."

"You didn't let him down, Charlie."

"And I need him to know that he can count on me, and I'll be there for him, and — and I love him." Charlie's words were coming out in a stream now, and tiny block tears fell down his face. "You know when the snake said, 'Love you lots, kiddo'? I hadn't heard my dad say that for a long time. He'd always say it after I told him I loved him, and the snake saying it made me realize how long it'd been since I said 'I love you' to my dad. I just want to tell him that again."

"Charlie. Look at me."

Charlie looked up.

"Your dad knows you love him, OK? He knows he can count on you too. Not only that, but we know we can count on you. You're gonna keep us safe through this level, and we're gonna see your dad soon."

"It's been a long time since I've played this level."

"You can do it. We trust you."

Charlie finally nodded. "OK. Follow me."

It took us nearly an hour to get through the level. Not only were there fire-breathing bats and lava floor tiles to deal with, but we also had to dodge raining fireballs, disappearing flame ghosts and, at one point, a tidal wave of boiling magma. Sometimes, Charlie would stand in place with his eyes closed for minutes on end, trying to remember the next part. Eric and I always waited patiently and followed his instructions exactly.

We all breathed a sigh of relief when we got to the end. Then Eric remembered something. "Wait, what are we going to do about the safe?"

CHAPTER FOURTEEN
Spiky Dungeon

Charlie lost the vote two-to-one. Eric sided with me — not so much because he wanted to get out of the game, but mostly because he wanted to see the last boss. Charlie shook his head. "I don't feel good about this, but I can't make you guys do something you don't want to do."

"Thanks for going along with this," I said. "And don't worry, it's gonna be OK."

I walked through the portal into the next level and instantly started to worry. This might not be OK. We were in a spiky-dungeon-themed level that played scary music. The level featured whirring saw blades, spike-covered wrecking balls and an army of sword-wielding skeletons — and that was just what I could see in front of me. But even scarier than those things were the glitches. The spinning blade, for example, was moving up and down. At the bottom of its path, it looked like a blocky, video game circle.

85

But about halfway up, it wobbled and glitched until it turned into a real whirring blade with hundreds of super-sharp teeth. I also noticed that blocks from the ground kept disappearing, reappearing and rearranging themselves into different patterns.

Charlie gulped. "Same thing as last time, guys. Follow me."

We timed our run past the saw blades, then rolled under the wrecking ball. When we got to the skeleton army, Eric pointed toward the ceiling. "How do we get that?" I looked up. It was an invincibility orb.

"Watch," Charlie said. He jumped onto the head of the first skeleton, then launched himself onto the second skeleton, which gave him the boost he needed to make it to the third skeleton. By the third skeleton, he'd built up so much speed and power that he was able to reach the invincibility orb. He grabbed it, ran back to us and presented it to Eric.

"Awesome!" Eric said as he prepared to push it into his chest. "You guys climb on my back, and I'll use this to run through the level!"

"No way," I said. "Bad things happen when we get in a hurry. Just hold onto it for now, and we'll use it in an emergency. Got it?"

"Hmf."

Unfortunately, the whole level was an emergency. Two different times, a chunk of spikes fell from the ceiling without warning. Another time, ten spinning blades appeared overhead and crashed to the ground all at once. We were always able to squeak through without using the invincibility, but our nerves were starting to fray.

And then there was the glitching. Every once in a while, we'd start feeling confident about our chances of making it through the dungeon alive. Then the ground would shake, the music would get all wobbly, and something weird would happen. One time, the level glitched while I was jumping over a pit of spikes, and the right side of my body turned real for a second. The pit wasn't long at all, but since my real body couldn't jump nearly as far as my video game body, I almost didn't make it. I had to grab the edge and pull myself up.

"How much farther?" I asked Charlie after the pit glitch.

"You're almost there," another voice said.

We all looked up at once to see Mr. Gregory waving to us from a platform near the ceiling. He had a real body and seemed to be glowing. From our perspective on the ground, he almost looked like an angel.

"Dad?!" Charlie yelled.

"Come up here quick, and I'll get you out of the game," Mr. Gregory said.

"Dad, I need to know if it's really you," Charlie said.

"Hurry, there's not much time," Mr. Gregory replied.

Charlie took a step toward the platform, and I grabbed his arm. "What if it's the RMG?"

"Then you'd better save my butt." With that, Charlie shook free and ran to the platform. "Dad, I'm sorry for messing up before, and I love you, and..."

"Wait, all three of you need to come up here!" Mr. Gregory said.

"I'm just making sure..." Charlie made it three steps away from the platform before getting knocked off his feet by another earthquake. The level glitched again, and suddenly the platform underneath Mr. Gregory disappeared. As Mr. Gregory fell to the ground, his real body turned into its video game form. We gasped when he finally hit the ground.

Lying in front of us was a metal skeleton with glowing, red eyes.

CHAPTER FIFTEEN
Glitchquake

Eric and I immediately got to work saving Charlie's butt. "The invincibility!" I yelled to Eric. "Now!"

Eric threw the glowing, yellow ball to Charlie. Or rather, he tried to throw it to Charlie. His missing elbow turned the toss into more of a catapult — a catapult that flung the ball onto the ground two feet in front of him.

"You had no problem throwing Charlie's entire body earlier!" I yelled.

"This is harder because it's smaller!"

I huffed, picked up the invincibility orb and tried throwing it with the same result.

While Eric and I struggled with the simple task of throwing a ball, Charlie had already scrambled onto a platform out of reach of the RMG. "Guys! Up here!"

By now, the RMG had started running toward

Eric and me. Without panicking, Eric backed up, got a running start and used my head as a springboard to jump up to the platform like he'd seen Charlie do. "Use the invincibility!" he yelled down to me.

I picked it up and was about to do just that when the RMG made an unexpected move. As soon as he got underneath Eric and Charlie's platform, he shot his arm into the air, grabbed the platform and grappled up. "He's coming!" I shouted.

The RMG swung himself onto the platform just as Eric and Charlie jumped off. I joined them, and we ran through the level. It took all my concentration to follow Charlie's lead as he slid under a spike that *shing*ed out of the wall, dodged a surprise guillotine that sliced the ground in front of us and jumped over a swordfish that leaped from a pit. (Why was there a swordfish inside a cave with no water? That is an excellent question that I did not get a chance to ask because I was too busy trying not to die.)

Just as we started putting distance between us and the RMG, the ground shook, and the level glitched again. We stopped to wait out the glitchquake like we had before but this one was worse. It just kept going and going. The ground in front of us began to crumble. I tried scrambling backward, but the shaking toppled me on top of Charlie. We both struggled to stand while the ground quaked and cracked, but we couldn't get our footing — it felt like trying to stand up on a trampoline when someone else is bouncing next to you. I dropped the invincibility orb and started crawling. The crumbling caught up to us, and just as the ground underneath my legs caved in, a hand yanked me away from the edge. I looked up to see that Eric had saved us.

"Thank you," I said when the shaking stopped.

"Don't thank me yet," Eric said, pointing to the enormous new pit in front of us.

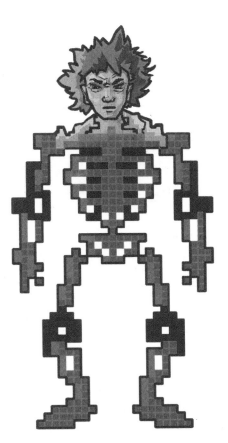

"No, you can thank him," another voice said. We all turned to see the RMG walking casually toward us. The glitchquake had caused his face to turn back to Mr. Gregory's, while his body remained a gray, video game robot skeleton. It was superduper terrifying. "I appreciate him keeping you safe so I can finish the job myself." The RMG's arm shot out, and his claw hand grabbed me.

Just then, one of the surprise guillotines from before fell from the ceiling and chopped the RMG's arm in half. The claw loosened its grip on me.

"Ha!" Eric laughed as he stepped forward. "Foiled again! Just when you think you got us…"

Eric couldn't finish his sentence because the RMG had shot out his other hand and grabbed Eric's throat. "Stop. Talking."

This was bad. This was very, very bad. I desperately searched for some way to rescue Eric, and that's when I noticed it. The invincibility orb lying on the ground, just out of reach.

The RMG picked Eric off the ground just like he'd done in Charlie's basement. "You have a big mouth. I can't wait to shut it for good."

I inched toward the yellow ball, slipped my oven mitt hand over it and started pulling it back to my body. I'd almost reeled it all the way in when the RMG noticed.

"HEY!" Still holding Eric, he shot his arm out even further and used it to scoop me in and pin me against his body.

"Please," Charlie pleaded, walking toward the

RMG. "Let them go."

"Charlie, Charlie, Charlie," the RMG shook his head. "We had such a good thing going."

"I'm the one you want, right?" Charlie said.

"We played catch, we told jokes — I was just like a real dad to you, wasn't I? Actually, I was always there for you, so I was kind of better than a real dad."

"Stop talking about my dad and tell me what you want."

"I want you to watch me kill your friends." The RMG's eyes glowed red, and his arm tightened around my chest. I couldn't breathe. I tried bringing the invincibility orb up to my chest, but he had my arm pinned tight. The world started going dark. Eric was yelling, Charlie was yelling, but the voices all started to blend together and fade. Then Charlie said something that snapped me out of it.

"DAD!"

I opened my eyes to see a giant blob behind Charlie. The snake again? I squinted to refocus and saw that it wasn't the snake, but a giant swordfish floating over the pit behind Charlie. The RMG looked surprised. "Wha..."

Before the RMG could finish that one-word question, the swordfish vaporized him with its own laser eyes. We heard a *BUM-BUM*, and the RMG disappeared.

"Wow!" Eric marveled. "Great timing! You really saved our bacon, Mr. Gregory!"

The swordfish looked at Eric and spoke. Its voice was much deeper and scarier than the snake's. "I'm not Mr. Gregory."

Then it jumped out of the pit and skewered all three of us at once.

CHAPTER SIXTEEN
Mr. Nice Guy

I flexed my arm. Touched my nose. Cracked my neck. Everything worked. I was either back in in the real world or in heaven.

I opened my eyes and immediately closed them. Too bright. Maybe it was heaven.

Clap. Clap. Clap.

I squinted and sat up. A doughy, middle-aged man wearing a t-shirt tucked into jeans stood over me, Eric and Charlie, clapping slowly. It was Max Reuben, the billionaire from TV.

CLAP-CLAP-CLAP.

Applause soon filled the room. The two dozen or so suits surrounding us followed their boss's lead and clapped like weirdos. I rubbed my eyes and tried to figure out where we'd ended up. The large, empty room looked like it had held dozens of office workers at one time, with carpet stains outlining cubicles and desks. The only thing in the room now was a tall, complicated tower right in the middle. It looked just like the one I'd seen at Mr. Gregory's Bionosoft lab, but in addition to the screens and lights from before, the tower also had wires leading to doors around the room. So many doors. At least 50 of them lined the four walls of the room, with a wire from each leading back to the tower.

The applause finally died down, and Max reached out his hand to help us up. "Hi! I'm Max from TV."

We got up without taking the hand. "Where's my dad?" Charlie demanded.

"He's here," Max said. "But we had to send him away while we tried to get you out of that rickety, old game. I'm glad you're safe now."

Charlie folded his arms and scowled. I admired his attempt at looking tough.

"Are you still upset about your dad?" Max asked. "I really needed him to work for me for a few weeks, but I didn't want you to be without a dad any longer. I knew he'd already left you alone recently."

Charlie stood silently with his arms folded, noticeably trembling.

"Wasn't the robot dad good enough for you?" Max asked. "I'd really hoped he would be."

"Why do you need Charlie's dad?" Eric asked.

"He's helping me with my big plan," Max said. Then his eyes lit up. "Do you want to hear the plan?"

"No!" I yelled. I'd seen enough movies to know that when the bad guy tells you his plan, it's all over. He has to kill you — those are the rules.

"Let's hear it," Eric said.

"No plan!" I yelled.

"Just a teensy bit of the plan?" Max fake-begged us.

"NO!"

"Yeah, sure, why not?" Eric said.

"ERIC!"

"Maybe it's a good plan," Eric whispered back.

Max rubbed his hands together. "Oh, it is a good plan! Now, where to begin? First…"

"NO PLAN!" I interrupted. That's all I got a chance to say before one of the suits put his giant hand over my mouth. "MMMM MFFF MFFFFFFFF!"

"Thank you, Daryl," Max said to the suit. "Also, before we go any further, I'd like to extend a proper welcome from all of us at the Max Investment

Agency headquarters in San Francisco, California. Welcome."

"Thank you!" Eric said. He actually seemed to be enjoying this. I couldn't understand what was wrong with him.

"We have one of the finest facilities in the city. I'd love to give you a tour sometime under better circumstances."

"Aw!" Eric whined. "No tour?"

"I have thousands of employees," Max said. "They are all wonderful people, but some might be — let's say — closed-minded to what we're doing here on the 56th floor."

"And what is it you're doing here?" Eric prodded.

Max smiled at me. "See, your friend..." He turned. "You're Eric, right?"

Eric grinned, proud that a billionaire knew his name. "Yep!"

"Your friend, Eric, is a delightfully open-minded individual. You should be more like Eric."

"People tell him that all the time," Eric said.

Max put his arm around Eric. "Eric, you know what I do, right?"

"Yeah, you're on that Shark Tank show."

Max gasped and pulled his hand back like Eric had just insulted his mother. "*LIONS' DEN!*" he shouted. "DON'T YOU EVER..." he stopped and composed himself. "I believe *Shark Tank* is vastly inferior to our show."

"Oh, of course. I think Lion Cave..."

"*LIONS' DEN!*"

"I think *Lions' Den* is way better too."

Max relaxed a little. "Exactly. While they're investing in toasters and scrub brushes, we're changing the world. A few years ago, I invested in a company that could not only change the world, but also the course of human history."

"Bionosoft?" Eric asked.

"Let me just say that you are a super-smart kid. Yes, Bionosoft. They were doing amazing things. That Hindenburg thing that creates perfect video game worlds by itself? Genius. A billion-dollar idea. The technology to transport people into video games? Maybe a trillion-dollar idea. The thing is — they were thinking small."

"Jevvrey Delfino told us about games that people could pay to live in," Eric said.

"Exactly. Just a little better virtual reality. Small potatoes," Max said. "But I kept pushing him to work on that because I had a plan of my own. Everything was almost ready when you two basically burned that company to the ground."

"We were just trying to help our friend," Eric pointed out.

"And no one could blame you for that," Max said. "Maybe it's my fault that they took Mark. I was pushing them pretty hard to finish. They took a few shortcuts and made some mistakes. But that's all OK now because my men were able to get Bionosoft's best asset out of the building before the police arrived."

He motioned to the door. Some suits on the other side must have been waiting for his signal because as soon as he motioned, two suits walked through with Mr. Gregory.

"DAD!" Charlie yelled. He tried to run, but a suit held him back.

Mr. Gregory looked defeated. His normally tall, pointy hair was droopy and disheveled. He looked like he hadn't shaved in a while, but instead of a regular beard, his face was covered with patches of wisps and stubble. His eyes got super sad when he saw us. "Why didn't you go into the safe?" he whispered with a hoarse voice.

Before we could reply, Max continued his speech. "Alistair Gregory here has been helping me put the finishing touches on my masterpiece for the last few weeks now."

"What is it?!" Eric asked, apparently unfazed by the appearance of Mr. Gregory. "What's the masterpiece?"

I'd finally had enough of Eric. Not only was he making friends with a supervillain who'd just admitted to kidnapping our friend's dad, but he was putting all of our lives in danger by keeping this maniac talking. I ripped the suit's hand off my mouth and yelled, "STOP! IF HE TELLS US, HE'LL HAVE TO KILL US!"

Max walked over to me and patted my back. "Is that what you're afraid of? Don't worry. I'm not going to tell you. I'm going to show you."

Just then, another door opened across the room. In stepped the fake mom I'd run into at the park earlier. Behind her were five suits surrounding a group of people. Charlie caught a glimpse of who they had before I did, and he started screaming. "NO! NO, PLEASE, NO!"

The suits parted long enough for me to see three children hugging a woman's leg.

Charlie crumpled. "MOM!"

CHAPTER SEVENTEEN
No More Mr. Nice Guy

Mr. Gregory ran toward his wife and kids, but the suits blocked his path. When he tried fighting through them, they pinned him down. Max approached Mr. Gregory, shaking his head. "I tried to play nice. You know that…"

"Excuse me!" Eric interrupted.

Max shot him an annoyed glance.

"How did they get here?" Eric asked.

"Who?"

"Them." Eric jabbed a finger toward Charlie's frightened family. "We live really far away from San Francisco, and they got here super-duper fast."

Max's annoyed expression turned to one of pride. "Oh, it's teleportation! I believe that's one you actually helped us with."

"Oh?" Eric looked proud to have contributed.

"Through your little *Go Wild* escapade, you showed us that this technology can be used for teleportation! Put someone in a video game over here, take him out over there. Another billion-dollar idea! Last week, Alistair helped us build quick-link teleportation doors to places around the world. We call them checkpoints." Max motioned to the doors lining the room. "Just another benefit of having this guy around." Max tussled Mr. Gregory's hair. Then he got serious as he turned his full attention to Mr. Gregory.

"Like I was saying, Alistair, you brought this upon yourself. If you'd finished our little project, I would have kept my promise. But a deal's a deal..."

"Where does this one go?" Eric interrupted again. He had worked his way over to the left wall and was holding one of the doors open. A blue glow from the other side lit up half his face.

"Close that!" Max yelled. A suit quickly slapped away Eric's hand and closed the door.

"Sorry," Eric said. "I just wanted to know where it goes."

Max looked annoyed again. "That one's Dubai, I think. But you can't be touching things in here!"

"Is Dubai near Washington D.C.?"

"What? No, it's in the Middle East."

"Do you have a door that goes to Washington D.C.?"

"This one!" Max banged the door behind him. "And if I hear one more word out of you, I'm going to tie you up, open this door, and throw you to the bottom of the Chesapeake Bay. Understand?!"

Eric nodded. He did not say another word.

Max turned back to Mr. Gregory. Eric's questions had erased the last of his patience. "Look, you've been telling me for weeks that the project's not ready. I think it is. So we're going to find out the hard way."

"Please," Mr. Gregory begged. "Just give me a little more time, and I promise..."

"No more Mr. Nice Guy," Max said. Then he turned, took a deep breath, put on the fake smile he'd been wearing earlier and walked toward Charlie's family. "Hi, kids!"

The kids all huddled closer to their mom.

Max got down on one knee. "Do any of you want superpowers?"

They didn't answer. They barely breathed. One of Charlie's sisters buried her face in her mom's leg.

"Don't be shy! Surely, you've thought about it before! You can have any superpower you want. Flying! Invisibility! Super strength! What'll it be?"

Silence for a second. Then, a small voice said, "Shar warsh?"

Max's face lit up, and he looked at Charlie's little brother, Christian. "Yes! Star Wars! Just like Star Wars! Do you want to be in Star Wars, young man?"

"Don't talk to him, Christian!" Mr. Gregory yelled.

Christian didn't talk, but he did give Max a slight head nod.

Max smiled even more. "Then Star Wars it is!" He grabbed Christian's hand. Charlie's mom lunged for him, but the suits held her back. Max walked Christian past Mr. Gregory, who was also struggling against two suits. "You want to get it ready, Alistair?"

"Max, please, it's not safe. If you just give me a few hours…"

"How about a few seconds?" Max retorted. He'd reached the other side of the room and threw open a door. This was the biggest door in the whole room — actually it was one of those double doors straight out of Dracula's castle. And instead of blue light coming from the other side, this light was swirling and red. Like lava. By now, Christian was having second thoughts. He tried to escape, but Max gripped his arm tighter.

"Max..." Mr. Gregory tried.

"Ten. Nine." Max started a slow countdown.

Mr. Gregory ran to the tower in the middle of the room and started furiously typing. "Wait! Just give me a minute!"

"Eight. Seven."

Mr. Gregory swiveled one of the screens up to his face. "It's not even booted up yet! He'll just burn up in there!"

"Six. Five."

Mr. Gregory dove to the other side of the tower. He unplugged one of the cables and moved it to another slot. A light started blinking on the tower, then three more lights lit up, and suddenly it *whooosh*ed.

"Four. Three."

Three screens came to life, showing a dusty, red planet.

"Two."

"Christian, Daddy loves you lots!" Mr. Gregory yelled.

"One."

"I'll get you out of there! Just don't…"

Before he could finish, Max threw the child into the red light and closed the door.

CHAPTER EIGHTEEN
Planet Bottomless Pit

For about ten seconds, everything was silent in the room. Mr. Gregory stared at one of the screens, so that's where everyone else looked too. Even the suits seemed nervous that Charlie wasn't going to make it. Finally, the screen flashed white, and a small boy appeared on the desert planet. The room breathed a sigh of relief. Mr. Gregory started checking screens and typing on three different keyboards at once.

Max walked by Mr. Gregory and gave him a sarcastic, extra-hard whack on the back. "Wow, works pretty well now, huh?"

"It's drawing too much power," Mr. Gregory said without looking up.

"Yeah I'm sure you'll figure it out," Max replied. "At least, you'd better figure it out. Because in 30 minutes, I'm throwing another one of your kids in there."

"In where?" Eric asked, breaking Max's "not-one-more-word" rule to ask a stupid question. "Where is he?"

"Eric, stop!" I yelled. "What is wrong with you?"

Max turned to me. "What, you're worried that I might reveal the rest of my plan, forcing me to kill you? Fine. I'll tell you."

Gulp.

Max pointed to the big door he'd just thrown Christian into. "That leads to the Reubenverse. It's a universe I've built with the help of an army of Hindenburgs. There's Planet Star Wars. There's Planet Lego. There's Planet of the Apes. There's Planet Eat-As-Much-Food-As-You-Want-Without-Getting-Sick. There's everything anyone could ever want in the Reubenverse, which is good because everyone's about to go there."

"When you say everyone..." Eric asked.

"The moment I give the word, everyone within 20 feet of a screen will automatically transport to the Reubenverse whether they want to go or not. I call it 'The Reuben Rapture.' With all the phones, computers and televisions in the world, we estimate we'll get 80 percent of the world's population on the first try."

I looked at Mr. Gregory, who was furiously typing to keep his son alive. "That's not possible, right?" I asked.

Max answered for Mr. Gregory. "It's possible if you have enough computer power — which I've bought — and the proper motivation for your talent," Max pointed to Christian on the screen. "Which I now have."

"Huh, neat idea," Eric said, apparently trying to butter up Max enough to become a prince or something in this new universe. "But why?"

"Hm, why would I want to create a universe where every president, king and dictator in the whole world has to answer to me? Why would I want to create a universe where I call every shot — who gets money, who gets food, who lives, who dies — based on how they treat me? Why would I want to create a universe where every dream I've ever had could come true in a second? I don't know. It's a tough call."

After that speech, I felt dizzy. Charlie's face was white. Mrs. Gregory had her eyes closed, and she was moving her mouth like she was praying. Half the suits looked like they were going to throw up, so apparently, this was the first time they'd heard the full scheme too. The only person who remained unaffected was Eric. He continued grinning like an idiot.

"Any other questions?" Max asked.

"That's all, thanks!" Eric answered.

Max turned to me and shrugged. "Then I guess I have no choice but to kill you." He gestured to the suits. "Let's try Planet Bottomless Pit."

The suits grabbed Eric, Charlie and I by the shoulders, but their grip wasn't as firm this time. They seemed really shaken up. I was shaken too, although not so much by the evil plan. I mean, the plan was evil to be sure. It was maybe the most evil plan I'd ever heard. I'd previously thought that blowing up the world was the worst thing a supervillain could do. But trapping humanity inside a video game so he could get some sort of sick pleasure out of it? That was next-level supervillainy.

No, the thing that had me reeling most was the betrayal of my best friend. Not only has Eric been my best friend for pretty much forever, but we've been through more together than probably any pair of friends on earth. Like, we took down an army of praying mantis aliens, and that wasn't even one of the 10 craziest things we'd done over the last five months. And then in five minutes, he'd thrown it all away — for what? I still wasn't sure. Did he think the Reubenverse was going to be cool or something? Even while we were being led to our Bottomless Pit of Doom, he still looked excited. What was wrong with him?

Then I saw it.

You know that moment in movies when the hero pieces everything together and time slows down? The footsteps always get echoey, and the camera zooms way in on a detail so small that no one could ever notice it without Superman vision and the ability to slow down time. I always thought that was just a dumb movie thing. It is not. It actually happened to me the moment I noticed that Eric was still wearing his dopey spy watch.

In real life, I shouldn't have been able to see more than that. But in super-slow-motion, zoomed-in movie mode, I noticed that a small, red recording light was blinking. Then I noticed the counter. Five minutes and four seconds.

Eric had recorded the whole thing.

CHAPTER NINETEEN
The White House

Eric noticed that I'd seen the watch and winked at me. I still couldn't figure out his plan — the recording wasn't going to do us much good tumbling down a bottomless pit. As it turned out, I didn't need to figure out what Eric had planned because he revealed it to everyone the second he stepped within grabbing range of the Washington D.C. door. As we passed the checkpoint, Eric shot out his hand and pulled the door right into his suit. Eric's suit stumbled for just a moment, which gave Eric enough time to squirm free, roll into the blue light and disappear.

Eric had escaped so fast that nobody had time to process what had happened. I felt my suit's grip loosen just a bit, which gave me the chance to wriggle free too. As soon as I got one foot into the light, I started getting sucked inside. I reached for Charlie, but his suit spun him away from me. "Charlie!" I kicked my legs to swim back out, but the force was too strong. The light sucked me in, tumbled me around a few times, then spit me onto a hardwood floor like a water slide.

Before I could figure out where I was, Eric's face appeared over my head. "Where's Charlie?!"

A hand appeared in the doorway — a beefy, certainly-not-Charlie-sized hand. Before the body that was attached to that hand could make it through, Eric slammed the door. At least, he tried to slam it. The door wouldn't quite close all the way thanks to the arm stuck in between.

"AHHHH!" someone screamed from the other side.

Even though Eric was pushing all his weight against the door, the arm squeezed farther in. Then a head *CLUNK*ed, and the door opened even more. I ran over, pushed the arm up with all my might and finally got it to slide back inside the blue. With the hand out of the way, Eric finally closed and locked the door.

Eric and I both slid to the ground to catch our breaths, which kicked up a plume of dust. We seemed to be in an old mansion like one of those you go to on boring field trips after they run out of cool places to visit. Once my eyes adjusted, I could tell we'd emerged from the closet of a giant, cobwebbed-filled bedroom.

"Is this the White House?!" Eric exclaimed.

"What? No. Do you really think they'd put one of these doors in the White House?"

"It's a mansion in Washington, D.C.! It's definitely the White House! Wow, what a lucky break this is!"

"It's not the White House! Look!" I dragged Eric to the window, and we peeked out. Our window overlooked a backyard overgrown with weeds and gnarled trees. By peeking around the corner, we could see that the house was covered with out-of-control ivy.

"Maybe it's the part of the White House you don't see," Eric suggested.

BANG!

We spun around to see the closet door start to buckle. "Can we get out of here now?!" I yelled.

BANG!

The door cracked a little. We ran out of the room and down a winding staircase. As we sprinted through the mansion's library, I tried to figure out Eric's plan. "Why did you want to come to Washington D.C.? Do you know someone here who can help us?"

"Yeah," Eric said, lagging behind because he kept trying to find secret passages by touching everything on the bookshelves. "We're going to play the recording for the one person who can help us."

"Great! Do you have a relative who works for the FBI or something?" I spotted the front door across the foyer and sprinted toward it. I unlocked the door just as we heard the *CRACK* of the closet door busting open and the *THOMP THOMP THOMP* of suits pouring into the bedroom. We sprinted outside to gray skies and a steady rain.

"No, we'll give it to someone even better," Eric said. "The President!"

I slammed on the brakes. "The what?!"

"The President! He's the only one powerful enough to take down Max Reuben!" Eric grinned. He was so proud of himself. My heart sank.

"Get in the bushes," I said, pushing Eric toward a thorny thicket next to the house.

"What? No, I — Ow! That hurts! Hang on, ow, ow!"

A suit emerged from the front door, and I put my hand over Eric's mouth. The suit looked both ways, spoke into his radio, then splashed down the street. A few seconds later, four more suits jogged outside and fanned through the neighborhood. Once things quieted down again, I turned to Eric and spoke as calmly as I could. "There is a zero percent chance that we reach the President without getting arrested or shot."

Eric shook his head. "Listen, we'll walk to the White House and play the clip for the Secret Service. Then we'll…"

I tuned out Eric and started fiddling with a golf ball in my pocket as I brainstormed ways to get us out of this mess. We could try playing the recording at FBI headquarters. Where was FBI headquarters? Actually, the Pentagon might be easier to find since it's shaped like a pentagon. Maybe we could…

I suddenly realized something and let out a gasp.

"Yeah!" Eric cheered. "I knew you'd like the idea!"

"No, I hate the idea," I said as I slowly took my hand out of my pocket.

"Then you must not understand it. See, all we have to do…"

"Eric," I interrupted. "I didn't have a golf ball in my pocket this morning."

"Uh, what?"

I opened my hand to reveal a glowing, yellow ball.

Now it was Eric's turn to gasp. "You still have that from the game?!"

"I guess I do." I stared at the ball in wonder when another realization hit me. "I know where we can play that recording."

"Where?!"

"We have to go back through the closet."

CHAPTER TWENTY
Dodo Doody

"Tell me the code word again," I instructed.

"Banana."

"Good. And you won't come in until you hear that, right?"

"Of course not."

"No matter what?"

"No matter what."

I nodded and said the thing that people say right before the last big action scene of a spy movie. "See you on the other side."

Eric fist-pounded me. "Ten-four, good buddy." He disappeared around the corner and started climbing the ivy. I waited until I heard him reach the awning, then edged my way to the front door. With any luck, all the suits would be out looking for us, which would leave the door unguarded.

When I reached the porch and peeked over the edge, I rediscovered that I have no luck. Two suits guarded the doorway. I slumped against the house and tried to figure out a new way inside. That's when I remembered *Dark Agent*, a spy video game Eric used to make me watch him play. In the game, Eric would sneak through room after room of guards by creating distractions. How would he distract these well-trained professionals? By throwing a can against the wall. "What was that?" the dumb video game guards would say. Then Eric would sneak behind their backs while they checked out the can.

"They fall for it every time!" I'd say. "This is so unrealistic."

"Jesse, this is how it works in the real world. They had an actual spy help them make the game, OK?"

With no other options, I decided to give it a shot. I didn't see any cans lying around, but there were plenty of rocks on the ground. I picked up one of the larger rocks, slipped back behind the bush and aimed for a big puddle on the sidewalk.

SPLOOSH!

"What was that?"

So far, so good. I waited for the suits to check out the sound, but they didn't move. Finally, I picked up another rock and tried again.

SPLOOSH!

This time, the suits saw the splash. But instead of checking it out, they followed the path of the rock's flight back to my bush. "There!" one of them said, pointing directly at me.

I knew video games were unrealistic. The suits ran down the stairs. "Where's the other one?!" they shouted. I tightened my grip on the invincibility, even though I knew it was way too early to use it. I needed to hold onto it until I got into the bedroom to give us enough time to make it through the door. When the suits ran off the porch, I tried to surprise them by running toward them.

One of the suits got down in a defensive basketball stance while the other guarded the sidewalk to keep me from running down the street. I ran harder, and as soon as I got to the basketball stance guy, I spun. He grabbed my arm, but the spin move yanked it away before he could pull me in. I slipped past the other suit, who thought I was going to try to run down the street, and sprinted into the house.

"You've got one coming inside," I heard one of them say over the radio. Great. Maybe he was only talking to one or two guys in the bedroom?

When I reached the foyer, I found that he was not talking to just one or two guys in the bedroom. He was talking to possibly every suit that Max Reuben had ever employed. They all stood on the steps with their guns drawn.

"Don't move, or we will shoot you," the suit up front said. The two suits from outside quickly ran in and closed the door behind me to cut off my escape. I slowly raised my hand to my chest.

"I SAID DON'T MOVE!" the suit repeated.

Now or never. I pressed the ball into my chest. It squished like a water balloon. I pushed harder until I felt a pop and immediately got warm.

Dodo doody doodoo doody-doody

I looked at my hands. They were glowing and singing the obnoxious invincibility tune.

BANG! BANG! BANG!

The sudden invincibility must have spooked the suits because they all opened fire at once. Their bullets just absorbed into my body.

Dodo doody

I smiled. Go time.

Doodoo doody-doody

I ran toward the stairs. Even though some of the

suits looked nervous, they held their ground and kept shooting. That was a very brave, very stupid move. I lowered my shoulder and plowed through the crowd like a bulldozer. One particularly large suit at the top of the stairs crouched down like he wanted to wrestle me, and I stiff-armed him into next week.

Dodo doody doodoo doody-doody

I turned right, then made a quick left into the bedroom. More suits. A lot more. The first one lunged for me, and I spun him behind my back through the door. The second one punched me in the face. I noticed that he seemed to be holding something back, probably because he felt bad about punching a 12-year-old in the face. I didn't feel a thing. I grabbed his arm and threw him through the ceiling into the attic.

"BANANA?!" I heard through the window.

"NOT YET!"

Dodo doody

A third suit had no qualms about assaulting a kid and punched me in the stomach as hard as he could. I didn't feel that either. He and I stared at each other for a second before I grabbed his arm and threw him through the hole in the ceiling that Suit #2 had created a moment earlier.

"WHAT ABOUT NOW?!" Eric was peeking through the window.

"JUST WAIT!"

doodoo doody-doody

The suits all rushed at once. Probably 20 of them piled on top of me, sneaking punches and trying to pin my arms. I waited patiently to give them all a chance to join the pile. I hadn't been keeping track of the invincibility, but it had to be almost over by now. Finally, I sprang up, catapulting all the suits through the wall and into the backyard.

Eric stared at me through the hole. "Can I come in now?"

"Yes!"

Eric remained still.

I rolled my eyes. "BANANA!"

He grinned and climbed into the room. "This is awesome! So I can punch you as hard as I want, and it won't hurt?"

Before I could answer, one more suit stepped through the closet door. This one carried a gun too, but it wasn't a normal gun like my friends on the stairs had. It was one of the plasma guns I'd seen at Bionosoft that could zap us straight to Planet

Bottomless Pit. He rolled for cover behind the bed and loaded a canister.

Dodo — Dodo — Dodo

My body started blinking as the invincibility wore off. "Eric! Curl into a ball!"

"Huh?"

I picked up Eric and used the last of my video game super strength to throw him as hard as I could just like I'd wanted to do in the first level of *Doom Island*. The suit popped up from behind the bed just in time to see Eric the Human Cannonball flying toward his face. He dropped the gun and raised his hands in self-defense, but it was no use — the cannonball won. Eric knocked the suit through the hole in the wall and picked up the plasma gun. "Let's go!"

We dove through the closet door just as the suits from the stairs started pouring into the bedroom. I tumbled a few times in the blue light, then rolled onto the floor of Max Reuben's headquarters. As soon as I hit the ground, I grabbed the door's power cord and yanked as hard as I could.

BWOWRRRrrrrr

The door powered down. Eric cracked it open to take a peek, then stepped aside so I could see. Just a wall. Good. I took a second to breathe and prepare myself to face a new onslaught of suits. How many were left? Twenty? Fifty?

I got the answer as soon as I turned. Zero.

The room was empty except for Mr. Gregory at the control tower and Charlie staring at us.

"Charlie!" I yelled. "So glad you're OK! Sorry for leaving you."

Charlie didn't say anything. He looked like he was going to throw up.

"Where did everyone go?"

Still nothing.

"It's OK," Eric said. "Jesse had a great idea! See, we're going to…"

"DON'T SAY ANYTHING!" Charlie yelled.

"Why? Nobody's here."

Charlie pointed at the control tower. I was confused. Mr. Gregory was the only one there. Just then, a second person poked his head around the other side of the control tower. My blood ran cold.

It was another Mr. Gregory.

CHAPTER TWENTY-ONE
Sparky the Squirrel Saves the Day

"Which one is the robot?!" Eric asked, pointing the plasma gun at the control tower.

"I don't know," Charlie said.

"You don't know?!" I asked. "It's the one who walked into the room while we were gone, right?"

"Yeah, but I never saw that happen because the whole room went bonkers when you guys disappeared. Those guys in suits started running everywhere. Max yelled something about a Code Black, then sent half of them after you and brought the other half with him. They grabbed my mom and sisters and left me alone in here with my dad and the robot."

We looked back at the control tower. The two Mr. Gregorys typed furiously on two different keyboards.

"I'm telling you for the last time, get your hand

off the keyboard!" Mr. Gregory #1 yelled.

"My son is in there!" Mr. Gregory #2 shot back.

"Hey!" Eric yelled.

Both Mr. Gregorys turned to us. Their eyes got big when they saw that Eric was pointing the plasma gun at them. "Eric, put that down," Mr. Gregory #1 said.

"Which one of you is the real Mr. Gregory?" Eric asked.

"I am," they both said at the exact same time, in the exact same tone.

"I'm keeping Christian alive, and he's trying to cook him in there by overclocking the processor," Mr. Gregory #2 said.

"No, listen. He's…"

Beep-Beep-Beep

One of the screens began flashing red.

"Oh no," Mr. Gregory #1 said. "Oh nonono." He ran to the screen and started punching buttons.

"Stop, he'll never make it!" Mr. Gregory #2 yelled as he hurdled a chair and tried to push Mr. Gregory #1 away from the keyboard.

Eric handed the gun to me. "Do something."

My mind raced. "Charlie, start asking them questions!"

"What book did you used to read me before bed?" Charlie shouted to the two Mr. Gregorys.

"Sparky the Squirrel Saves the Day," they both answered at once.

"Where did I want to eat my birthday meal every year when I was little?"

"The Subway at Walmart." Again, both Mr. Gregorys gave the same answer at almost the same time. Whichever one was the robot must have had such a good computer brain that it could copy the real Mr. Gregory's answer in a millisecond.

"Jesse!" Mr. Gregory #2 said. "If you don't act fast, Christian is going to burn up in there. Please!"

I breathed faster and tried to concentrate on the blinks. One-two-three-blink. I looked at the other Mr. Gregory. One-two-blink.

Bee-bee-bee-beep! Bee-bee-bee-beep!

The tower beeped faster. Both Mr. Gregorys went back to their computers on opposite sides of the tower. "Christian has maybe a minute left!" Mr. Gregory #1 said.

I looked over Mr. Gregory #2's shoulder to try to figure out the computer code gibberish. I'd never taken a programming class in my life — how was I supposed to know if this Mr. Gregory's code was the one saving Christian or killing him? I tried to keep up with the commands streaming down the screen as Mr. Gregory's fingers flew across the keyboard. Wait a second. I shifted my attention from the screen to Mr. Gregory's fingers. They were typing fast. Faster than I'd seen anyone type in my life. Maybe faster than a human could type. I raised the plasma gun.

BEEEEEEEEEEEP! BEEEEEEEEEEEEP!

"Jesse," Charlie whispered, pushing my gun down.

"I got it," I whispered back.

"I need to do this," Charlie said, stepping in front of the gun.

I tried to move around Charlie. "I have a good shot! Get out of the way."

Charlie moved with me. He was holding out his hands. "Jesse, give it to me. I need to be the one that pulls the trigger."

"But…"

"Please." His voice cracked. "That's my dad and brother, not yours."

The way he said that last sentence made me stop and rethink everything I'd done that day. I'd seen myself as the hero by rescuing us from the RMG in the basement and then choosing to bypass the safe. But from Charlie's point of view, every decision I'd made had put his family in greater danger. I handed Charlie the gun.

"Dad," Charlie said. Both Mr. Gregorys stopped what they were doing and turned to him. Charlie pointed the gun at Mr. Gregory #2 and looked at Mr. Gregory #1. "Love you," he said.

Mr. Gregory #1 nodded. "You've made the right decision, son."

Just before Charlie could pull the trigger, Mr. Gregory #2 spoke up. He didn't try to plead for his life or convince Charlie that he was wrong. He just said four words.

"Love you lots, kiddo."

That was all Charlie needed to hear. He smiled, then spun and blasted Mr. Gregory #1.

CHAPTER TWENTY-TWO
Escape

Mr. Gregory #1 opened his mouth when the blast hit him, but he never got a chance to make a sound. His body flashed once, revealing a metal skeleton, then disappeared for good.

Eric stared at Charlie with his mouth open. "You almost blasted your real dad into a bottomless pit!"

Mr. Gregory hugged his son. "He knew what he was doing."

BLEEEEEEEEEEEEEEEEEP!

The tower screeched to remind us that Christian was still inside, and Mr. Gregory ran back to his keyboard. After just a few keystrokes, the noise stopped, and Mr. Gregory breathed a sigh of relief.

Charlie hugged Eric and me. Neither of us is very huggy, so we patted Charlie on the back awkwardly while he thanked us. "My brother would be gone right now if it weren't for you two." He finally let go and smiled. "How did you know to come back?"

Oh yeah! I'd forgotten all about the real reason we'd returned. "Eric! The watch!"

Eric took the spy watch off his wrist. "Mr. Gregory, does this building have an intercom system?"

"Yes, through the phones. Why?"

Eric motioned to me, and I explained. "Eric recorded Max Reuben's whole plan. If we try to bring it to the police ourselves, Max will probably just send more suits like he did last time. But there's no way he can stop the message from getting to the police if we play it for the whole building."

"That's brilliant!" Mr. Gregory said, leaping into action. He punched a series of numbers into a phone next to the control tower and held the receiver to his mouth. "Attention, employees of Max Investment Agency." His voice echoed over the intercom speakers in the ceiling. "This is Alistair Gregory speaking to you from the 56th floor. I'm sure many of you have wondered about Max Reuben's secret project. I'm here to tell you that it's bad. The next voice you will hear is Max himself confessing."

Eric handed over his watch, and Mr. Gregory pressed, "PLAY."

"I have thousands of employees," Max's voice played over the intercom speakers. "They are all wonderful people, but some might be — let's say — closed-minded to what we're doing here on the 56th floor."

As the recording played, Mr. Gregory went back to his keyboard. "I might have figured out a way to get Christian out. Charlie, can you help me on the other keyboard? When I give the word, I need you to hold down the 'ESCAPE' key, OK? Three, two…"

BANG! BANG! BANG!

The countdown got interrupted by loud knocking. We all turned. The knocking came from the hallway door Max and his goons had run through. Before we could run back to protect the watch, the door swung open, and Mrs. Gregory and the kids tumbled through.

"Daddy! Daddy!" The Gregory girls ran over and clutched their father's leg.

Mr. Gregory hugged his wife. "How did you escape?"

"When that recording started playing, the men who were guarding us ran away," Mrs. Gregory said. "Is Christian OK?"

"Better than OK! I'm about to bring him back.

Ready, Charlie?"

"Ready."

Mr. Gregory typed a few commands on his keyboard. "Hit it!"

Charlie pressed the "ESCAPE" key, and the Reubenverse door lit up. It glowed brighter and brighter until little Christian Gregory tumbled out, holding what appeared to be a real lightsaber. Christian blinked a few times, then looked down to see what he was holding in his hand. "SHAR WARSH!" he yelled, holding the lightsaber above his head.

"Christian, put that down right now!" Mrs. Gregory commanded.

Christian obeyed, and the whole family swallowed him up in a hug. "Are you guys ready to go home?" Mr. Gregory finally asked, opening one of the checkpoint doors.

Mrs. Gregory eyed the blue light skeptically. "Is this safe, hon?"

Before Mr. Gregory could answer, Christian had picked the lightsaber back up and walked through the door. "WAIT! NOT IN THE HOUSE!" Mrs. Gregory yelled as she sprinted after him. Charlie held his sisters' hands and walked through too.

I turned to Mr. Gregory. "Aren't you going?"

He shook his head sadly. "I have to stay behind and clean up this mess. I just wish I could go back in time and make myself drop this whole thing. I put so many people in danger."

"This isn't your fault," I said. "You made something awesome, and people used it for bad stuff."

"Like the guy who invented bazookas," Eric offered helpfully.

"I can't thank you both enough," Mr. Gregory said. "Without your help, my family might never have made it."

"Any time you want to put us in a video game, we're ready," Eric said.

"Nobody's ever going in a video game again," Mr. Gregory said. "Now let's get you home."

Eric and I started to walk through the door the Gregory family had gone through. "No, not there," Mr. Gregory said. "I can get you even closer."

He led us to a nearby door. "They built one that goes to your basement, Eric."

"Creepy," I said.

"Cool!" Eric said at the same time.

Eric stepped into the blue, then I followed. After a few seconds of falling, I tumbled out of Eric's TV onto his ratty basement carpet.

CHAPTER TWENTY-THREE
Code Black

We had played it cool with Mr. Gregory, but alone in Eric's basement, we let loose. "WOOOOO!" Eric beat his chest like Tarzan while I jumped up and down.

"Can you believe it?!" I yelled. "We were like superspies!"

"Zero zero seven, at your service," Eric said, tilting pretend sunglasses on his face.

"I think it's 'double-oh-seven,'" I said.

"What?"

"Never mind. Hey, turn on the news. I want to see if the FBI is at Max Reuben's building yet."

"Great idea!" Eric said, turning to search the couch for the remote.

I sprawled out on the carpet and closed my eyes. I'd already been to San Francisco, Washington D.C.

and the jungles of a 1980s video game, and it wasn't even noon yet.

Eric pointed a remote at the TV and tried a few buttons. "That's not it..." he muttered.

I thought back to our watch scheme and shook my head. It really wasn't that great of a plan. If any suits had been in the room when we'd returned from Washington D.C. or even if they'd have barged in while the recording was playing, everything would have fallen apart. I paused and thought about it some more. "Hey Eric, don't you think it's weird that Max just let us play that recording without trying to stop us?"

"Hm?"

I turned around. Eric was too busy smelling a gummy worm he'd found between the cushions of his couch to pay attention.

"Like, why did Max just leave and not come back? They had cameras in there, right? I'm sure they saw us come back in."

Eric was now trying to chew the gummy worm. "Who knows," he said. "Hey, can you pick up that side of the couch? I think the TV remote is down there."

I picked up the couch, then immediately dropped

it. "Code Black!"

"Hey!" Eric yelled. "You can't just drop that without warning! I could have been under there!"

"Remember Charlie saying that Max had said something about a Code Black when he left the room?"

"So what?"

"So what if Max didn't care about stopping us because he had a backup plan?"

"Or what if he was just running away?" Eric asked. "Can you stop worrying long enough to pick up the couch?"

Just then, the TV turned on by itself. A blurry image appeared for a second, then the picture snapped into focus. It was Mr. Gregory.

"Jesse! Eric! We've got a problem!" Mr. Gregory was still in the control tower room, but now lights and sirens were going off behind him.

"What's the matter?"

"I don't know how he did it, but he did it!"

"Did what?!"

"I need you back here right now! Can you find a controller?"

Eric and I grabbed two controllers from the TV stand.

"I'm sorry," Mr. Gregory said as he typed something. "So, so sorry."

The controller rumbled in my hands, and the room went black. As I fell into the darkness, flashing red lights started to appear. Also, there was a voice. It was the same friendly woman's voice that chirps, "Tenth floor!" on elevators. Except this particular voice had a much more terrifying message.

"Ten minutes to rapture."

A Note from the Author

I know! I know. That was a very mean place to end the story. Don't worry, I'll be releasing Trapped in a Video Game: Book Five – the last book in the series – very soon. To get updates on that book, a heads up as soon as it's available on Amazon and other cool stuff, enter your email address at dustinbradybooks.com.

Thank you for taking the time to read *Trapped in a Video Game: Book Four.* If you liked this book, please consider telling your friends or posting a short review on Amazon. Word of mouth is an author's best friend and much appreciated.

If you want to get in touch with me for any reason, I'd love to hear from you! You can email me any time at dustin@dustinbradybooks.com.

Thanks again for reading my book!

ABOUT THE AUTHOR
Dustin Brady

Dustin Brady hails from the world-renowned City of Champions (Cleveland, Ohio). He has spent a good chunk of his life getting crushed over and over in *Super Smash Brothers* by his brother Jesse and friend Eric.

ABOUT THE ILLUSTRATOR
Jesse Brady

Jesse Brady is a professional illustrator and animator in Pensacola, Florida. If he got trapped in a Mega Man video game, he would totally dominate.

Made in the USA
Columbia, SC
22 January 2018